WEDDING WORDS

VOWS

JENNIFER CEGIELSKI

Stewart, Tabori & Chang
New York

Published in 2005 by
Stewart, Tabori & Chang
115 West 18th Street
New York, NY 10011
www.abramsbooks.com

Library of Congress Cataloging-in-Publication Data

Cegielski, Jennifer.
  Wedding words : vows / by Jennifer Cegielski.
    p. cm.
  Includes bibliographical references and index.
  ISBN 1-58479-428-3 (alk. paper)
  1. Marriage service. I. Title.

BL619.M37C44 2005
203'.85—dc22

                          2005010895

Editor: Beth Huseman
Designer: Studio Blue, Chicago
Production Manager: Jane Searle

The text of this book was composed in Hoefler Text.

Printed in China

10 9 8 7 6 5 4 3 2 1
First Printing

Stewart, Tabori & Chang is a subsidiary of

LA MARTINIÈRE

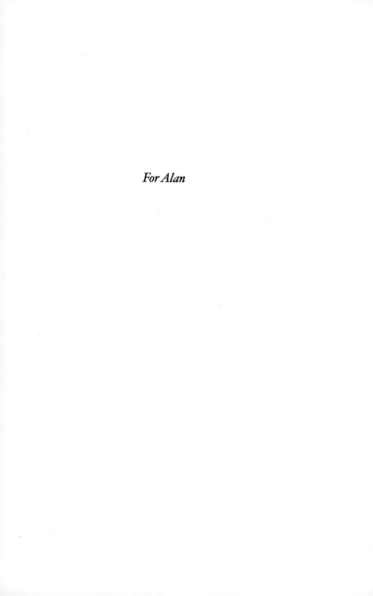

For Alan

Contents

The consciousness of loving and being loved
brings a warmth and richness to life
that nothing else can bring.

—OSCAR WILDE

INTRODUCTION

IT IS EASY TO GET swept up in the whirlwind of planning a wedding. There is hardly a shortage of preparation, coordination, and seemingly endless decisions. What are you going to wear? Where will you celebrate your reception? Should you choose platinum or gold for your rings? Where will you spend your honeymoon? There's no denying these decisions are a fun and exciting part of the planning process. But take a moment and consider this: the most important elements of your wedding can't be worn, booked, or bought. They are the vows spoken by you and your partner, and the foundation of your union.

A wedding vow is a promise of your love and a pledge to your future with another person. It is made freely and spoken publicly. Depending on the type of wedding ceremony you will have, the actual words of your vows may be determined by your religion, your culture, or your government, or you may even choose to scribe your own. Regardless of where they come from, no other words you will ever say will be weighed with so much meaning or fill you with so much emotion. Perhaps this is because it is so rare that we as human beings ever say something so binding directly to another individual, out loud and looking deeply into his or her eyes. "I'm choosing you, above all others, to spend my life with me" is a strong statement, and the words create a bond that in essence transcends your existence.

One theory about the custom of wedding vows puts its origins in an Ancient Roman ritual, when a couple would hold hands and make a pledge in the presence of a priest or priestess following an animal sacrifice. While thankfully no modern-day four-legged friends need give up their lives in order for you to tie the knot, the requirement to make your pledge in the presence of company still stands in order to make you "married" in the eyes of the law. In addition to your chosen family and friends, your vows are witnessed by an officiant of some sort for a religious or spiritual ceremony, a judge or other such authorized person for a non-denominational or civil ceremony, and sometimes specific individuals or sponsors as deemed by religious or cultural aspects of your wedding.

It would be an oversight when talking about wedding vows not to mention where they fall in the proceedings overall. In the course of most wedding ceremonies, the vows are at the heart, both literally and figuratively. Once they have been pledged the couple is truly considered married. Within many ceremonies, there is also declaration of consent or intent prior to the vows: You are there of your free will, with the desire to wed the other person. Many ceremonies also include a vow or statement given when rings are exchanged.

Western religious weddings follow something along the lines of the format below, while civil ceremonies follow a similar structure, minus the prayers and religious readings:

Processional
Greeting/Statement of purpose
Opening prayers
Readings
Declaration of consent/intent
VOWS
Ring exchange
Pronouncement of marriage
Kiss
Blessing
Recessional

Whatever path you choose to take down the aisle—be it spiritual, secular, or somewhere in between—what remains at the end of the day (and from that day forward) is the enduring testament to your love. The words you say may be the same as those pledged by generations of couples before you, or they may come directly from your own hand and heart. In this book, you'll find examples of traditional vows as well as guidelines for writing your own, plus some public speaking tips for the actual delivery. A selection of quotes, poems, and words of devotion from artists, writers, and lovers through the ages are included to inspire you as you compose your own vows, prepare readings and programs, or even serve as food for thought as you contemplate the momentous promise the two of you are about to make.

What a grand thing to be loved!
What a grander thing still, to love!
—VICTOR HUGO

CHAPTER ONE

VOW FORM AND FUNCTION

WHILE IT'S TRUE that wedding vows vary from faith to faith and couple to couple, there is some pattern to their content and structure. All vows essentially include a statement that you are free and willing to marry, a declaration to love one another, and pledges to uphold one another and grow together as you accept the changes that occur throughout your lives. If you will be saying a pre-existing vow from your faith or a vow for a civil service, it is helpful to acquaint yourself with its format in advance. If you will be writing your own vows, you should agree on the format you will both use. Traditional Western wedding vows take on an array of different formats. Here are a few of the more familiar versions.

Statement or Monologue Vows

As the name suggests, each person makes a singular statement with this type of vow. When the words are essentially the same (substituting husband/wife and his/her) for both parties they are called mutual vows; these are the most common. Alternatively, there may be two different statements created, with one read by each individual. In a statement vow, there is a subtle build in importance of the things said, starting with an introduction, then moving into the body, and ending with a conclusion.

The sample structure below is fairly traditional. For vows you write yourself, you might include some personal reflection—what your life was like before you met this person, your feelings on marriage, your happiness at the arrival of this day—or something about your future spouse's significance—a recollection of your first feelings of love for him or her, the traits and characteristics of this person you value, how your partner has impacted your life or makes you feel about yourself.

Sample structure:

INTRODUCTION

Declaration of Intent
"I, [name], take you [name],"

While clearly by this point you know each other's names, this simple statement sets the record straight to all who hear that you have arrived at this occasion of your own free will and are choosing your partner specifically. Depending on your preference and level of formality of your wedding, use full names or first names only.

Definition of Your Relationship
For example, "to be my lawfully wedded husband/wife" or "to be my partner in our lifelong journey together."

BODY

Your Promises
What tenets will you uphold in your marriage? Often, these are preceded by resolute verbs like "will," "promise," or "pledge." There is no mystery to these promises. At their most basic, they are the foundation of most good and lasting relationships: to honor and cherish each other; to respect each other's individuality; to be kind and understanding; to be honest and faithful; to be a good friend.

Circumstances and Duration
It is in this part of the vow that you acknowledge that life is always changing, in both positive and less positive

ways. The traditional circumstances address "in sickness and in health, for richer for poorer," while a more contemporary vow might say, "wherever our lives may take us." Despite these changes, you vow that your union will endure. Some traditional vows often set a point of termination of "to death do us part," while a contemporary vow might use the less ominous "all the days of our lives" or "as long as we both shall live." If you feel your love transcends mere mortal limits, add on the clause of "and for all eternity" or even "forever."

CONCLUSION

Generally there is a final statement to signify the end of the vow.
"This is my solemn vow."
"From this day forward, I pledge all these things to you."

Dialogue or Exchange Vows

In this version, the couple recites one vow, with each partner speaking alternate lines or paragraphs. The couple may use the pronouns "I" or "we" depending on the set up of the vow. When recited, this vow might almost resemble a story in the way it is told and how each person has a particular role. Loosely structured with the same combination of introduction-body-conclusion as a statement vow, this is a more unusual and contemporary style of vow and perhaps the most collaborative.

Sample structure:

INTRODUCTION

Declaration of Intent
BRIDE: "Today before our family and friends,"
GROOM: "we declare our love for one another."

Definition of Your Relationship
BRIDE: "I choose you for my husband."
GROOM: "I choose you for my wife."

BODY

Your Promises
BRIDE: "We will be faithful partners."
GROOM: "We will honor each other."
BRIDE: "We will comfort each other."
GROOM: "We will share our hopes and dreams,"

Circumstances and Duration
BRIDE: "through good times and bad."

GROOM: "From this day forward."

CONCLUSION

BRIDE AND GROOM (together): "This is our solemn vow."

Interrogative or Question-and-Response Vows

This vow requires the participation of the officiant, who addresses the first person by name and asks a series of questions to which the person responds, "I do" or "I will"; this process is then repeated by the officiant with the second person. The example below is very traditional, but depending on the questions in the body section of the vows, this style could also sound very contemporary.

Sample structure:

INTRODUCTION

Declaration of Intent and Definition of Your Relationship
OFFICIANT: "[Name], do you take [name] to be your husband/wife?"

Your Promises
OFFICIANT: "Do you promise to love him/her, comfort him/her, honor and keep him/her"

Circumstances and Duration
OFFICIANT: "in sickness and in health, for better or for worse, all the days of your lives?"

CONCLUSION/RESPONSE

BRIDE/GROOM: "I do."

An officiant may assist in the delivery of vows by "directing" them. That is, he or she states the phrases or sentences from the vow, which would then be repeated by the person reciting them; the officiant would then repeat the process with the other person.

In some ceremonies the officiant will lead a group response to the vows, where friends and relatives affirm that they bless and support the union. The officiant might say something along the lines of, "Who will support and encourage this couple in the commitment they are about to make?" and the group of witnesses assembled would answer, "We will."

*There is no more lovely, friendly, and charming relationship,
communion or company than a good marriage.*

—MARTIN LUTHER

CHAPTER TWO

RELIGIOUS AND SPIRITUAL VOWS, PRAYERS, AND BLESSINGS

THE VALUES AND MORES set forth by the world's religions have long provided a foundation to make the wedding ceremony a sacred experience. Several faiths regard marriage as an important act between two people; some consider it a covenant, while others look upon it as a duty or even a holy obligation in terms of ensuring future generations of like believers. And while no one belief system holds the monopoly on the wording of wedding vows, it is interesting to note the similarities of the sentiments from faith to faith. Promises to stay together as your relationship may change and as life throws you curveballs with regards to happiness, health, and wealth are common denominators across the board.

Though the majority of these vows are fairly simple in their language and traditional in their delivery, they eloquently state the key promises for a successful marriage. The vows are generally preceded by a declaration of intent or consent (some have been included in the following examples). Couples who choose to state the vows of their faith can cherish the fact that these very same pledges have sealed unions for generations. The vows make inspiring reading whether you are a believer or a non-believer and whether you are following your own faith's traditions together, intermingling your own beliefs with those of your future spouse in an interfaith ceremony (see page 20), or are taking a more secular approach to the proceedings.

Please note that the wordings provided here tend to be the most common, but you may wish to double check with your clergy member or officiant for any variations as deemed appropriate by your particular house of worship. In addition, if you wish to stay within the guidelines of your faith while injecting some of your own personality into your promises, discuss the possibility of supplementing these vows with a few sentences you have written yourself.

Baha'i

This simple statement is recited by the bride and groom before witnesses from their spiritual assembly.

We will all, verily, abide by the will of God.

Buddhist

In countries where Buddhism is widely practiced, weddings are a social convention, not a religious one. While Buddhist monks do not preside over wedding ceremonies in the way a Western priest or rabbi might, they may offer wedding blessings (which can vary from order to order and temple to temple) or chant before or after the ceremony. There are no set wedding vows, but the bride and groom may recite the traditional undertakings expected of them as found in the sacred text Sigilovdda Sutta:

GROOM: Towards my wife I undertake to love and respect her, be kind and considerate, be faithful, delegate domestic management, provide gifts to please her.

BRIDE: Towards my husband I undertake to perform my household duties efficiently, be hospitable to our kin and friends, be faithful, protect and invest our earn-

ings, discharge my responsibilities lovingly and consci-
entiously.

Christian

*The numerous divisions of Christianity each have their
own version of wedding vows.*

~~~~~~~~
AMISH
~~~~~~~~

*There are several practicing Amish communities through-
out the United States, and many have specific wording for
their vows. Here is one of the most common, from the Old
Order Amish sect:*

Do you acknowledge and confess also that it is a Christian order that there should be one husband and one
wife, and can you have the confidence that you have
begun this undertaking in the way you have been
taught? *Yes.*

Do you also have the confidence, brother, that the Lord
has ordained this our fellow sister to be your wedded
wife? *Yes.*

Do you also have the confidence, sister, that the Lord
has ordained this our fellow brother to be your wedded

husband? *Yes.*

Do you solemnly promise your wife that if she should be afflicted with bodily weakness, sickness, or some such similar circumstances that you will care for her as is fitting for a Christian husband? *Yes.*

And do you likewise promise the same to your husband, that if he should be afflicted with bodily weakness, sickness, or some similar circumstances, that you will care for him as is fitting for a Christian wife? *Yes.*

Do you solemnly promise with one another that you will love and bear and be patient with each other and not separate from each other until the dear God shall part you from each other through death? *Yes.*

BAPTIST

Within the Baptist church there are many denominations, and each has the ability to determine the words used for wedding vows. Typical vows from this faith might read:

Will you, [name], have [name] to be your wife? Will you love her, comfort and keep her, and forsaking all others remain true to her, as long as you both shall live? *I will.*

Will you, [name], have [name] to be your husband? Will you love him, comfort and keep him, and forsaking all others remain true to him, as long as you both shall live? *I will.*

I, [name], take thee, [name], to be my wife, and before God and these witnesses I promise to be a faithful and true husband.

I, [name], take thee, [name], to be my husband, and before God and these witnesses I promise to be a faithful and true wife.

EASTERN ORTHODOX

The wedding ceremony of this faith is longer than most, with several symbolic rituals including a betrothal where the bride's and groom's wedding bands are exchanged three times and a crowning of wreaths. No vows are spoken verbally by the couple. The couple is considered married when the crowns are removed by the priest with the blessing:

Be thou magnified, O bridegroom.

MENNONITE

Like the Amish, the Mennonites vary wedding vow wording from sect to sect. This is an example of one of the more widely-used vows:

Do you believe that matrimony is an ordinance instituted of God, and confirmed and sanctioned by Jesus Christ, and that you must therefore enter upon it in the fear of God? *I do.*

Do you confess and declare that you are unmarried, and free from all other marriage relations and engagements whatsoever? *I am.*

Will you, in the presence of God, and these witnesses, take [name], the sister by your side, to be your wedded wife; will you love and cherish her, provide and care for her in health and sickness, in prosperity and adversity, exercise patience, kindness, and forbearance toward her, live with her in peace as becometh a faithful Christian husband; and, forsaking all others, keep yourself only unto her as long as you both shall live? *I will.*

Will you, in the presence of God, and these witnesses, take [name], the brother by your side, to be your wedded husband; will you love and cherish him in health and in sickness, in prosperity and adversity, share with him the joys and sorrows of life, exercise patience, kindness, and forbearance toward him, live with him in peace as becometh a faithful wife; and, forsaking all others, keep yourself only unto him as long as you both shall live? *I will.*

Option I

In the name of God, I, [name], take you, [name], to be my wife, to have and to hold from this day forward, for better, for worse, for richer, for poorer, in sickness and in health, to love and to cherish, until we are parted by death. This is my solemn vow.

In the name of God, I, [name], take you, [name], to be my husband, to have and to hold from this day forward, for better, for worse, for richer, for poorer, in sickness and in health, to love and to cherish, until we are parted by death. This is my solemn vow.

Option II

Will you have this woman to be your wife, to live together in a holy marriage? Will you love her, comfort her, honor and keep her in sickness and in health, and forsaking all others, be faithful to her as long as you both shall live? *I will.*

Will you have this man to be your husband, to live together in a holy marriage? Will you love him, comfort him, honor and keep him in sickness and in health, and forsaking all others, be faithful to him as long as you both shall live? *I will.*

The various branches of Protestantism all have their own interpretations of the wedding vow.

ANGLICAN/EPISCOPAL

In the Name of God, I, [name], take you, [name], to be my wife, to have and to hold from this day forward, for better for worse, for richer for poorer, in sickness and in health, to love and to cherish, until we are parted by death. This is my solemn vow.

In the Name of God, I, [name], take you, [name], to be my husband, to have and to hold from this day forward, for better for worse, for richer for poorer, in sickness and in health, to love and to cherish, until we are parted by death. This is my solemn vow.

LUTHERAN

In the presence of God and this community, I, [name], take you, [name], to be my wife; to have and to hold from this day forward, in joy and in sorrow, in plenty and in want, in sickness and in health, to love and to cherish, as long as we both shall live. This is my solemn vow.

In the presence of God and this community, I, [name], take you, [name], to be my husband; to have and to hold from this day forward, in joy and in sorrow, in plenty and in want, in sickness and in health, to love and to cherish, as long as we both shall live. This is my solemn vow.

PRESBYTERIAN

Option I

I [name], take you, [name], to be my wife; and I promise before God and these witnesses, to be your loving and faithful husband; in plenty and in want; in joy and in sorrow; in sickness and in health; as long as we both shall live.

I [name], take you, [name], to be my husband; and I promise before God and these witnesses, to be your loving and faithful wife; in plenty and in want; in joy and in sorrow; in sickness and in health; as long as we both shall live.

Option II

Before God and these witnesses I [name], take you, [name], to be my wife, and I promise to love you, and to be faithful to you, as long as we both shall live.

Before God and these witnesses I [name], take you, [name], to be my husband, and I promise to love you, and to be faithful to you, as long as we both shall live.

For a wedding without any religious or spiritual overtones at all, a civil ceremony might be the answer. A civil ceremony can be performed at a city hall or pretty much anywhere by a judge, attorney, notary, mayor, or anyone legally authorized to solemnize a marriage. Wording of civil vows can vary from state to state, but they sound something like this:

I, [name], take you, [name], to be my lawfully wedded wife. I promise from this day forward to be your faithful husband, for better for worse, for richer for poorer, in sickness and in health, to love and to cherish as long as we both shall live.

I, [name], take you, [name], to be my lawfully wedded husband. I promise from this day forward to be your faithful wife, for better for worse, for richer for poorer, in sickness and in health, to love and to cherish as long as we both shall live.

How does a couple from two different religious backgrounds prepare for their wedding ceremony and vows? If you wish to have a religious ceremony, the first thing to do is to check with your respective church or temple about restrictions, as some faiths will not support mixed unions or perform ceremonies for couples of mixed faiths. If yours will, you might wish to work with officiants from each faith to incorporate both traditions into your vows, and choose to have the ceremony in the house of worship of one faith or, if allowed, neutral territory such as a restaurant or reception location.

Alternatively, you may decide to work with an interfaith minister to create customized vows and an interfaith wedding ceremony. This type of ceremony is also a good option when one person comes from a religious background and his or her partner does not, or when you wish to have a ceremony that is still spiritual without being overly religious. A good interfaith minister will work with you to develop vows that are a meaningful reflection of your relationship and your beliefs. See Further Reading on page 145 for where you can find more information about interfaith weddings.

QUAKER

A Quaker wedding takes place in front of the congregation during a regular meeting, and is not presided over by an officiant. In addition, many Friends prefer the term "promise" to "vow" because of their historical opposition to oath taking.

In the presence of God and these our friends, I, [name], take thee, [name], to be my wife, promising with Divine assistance to be unto thee a loving and faithful husband so long as we both shall live.

In the presence of God and these our friends, I, [name], take thee, [name], to be my husband, promising with Divine assistance to be unto thee a loving and faithful wife so long as we both shall live.

ROMAN CATHOLIC

Option I

I, [name], take you, [name], to be my wife. I promise to be true to you in good times and in bad, in sickness and in health. I will love you and honor you all the days of my life.

I, [name], take you, [name], be my husband. I promise to be true to you in good times and in bad, in sickness and in health. I will love you and honor you all the days of my life.

Option II
I, [name], take you, [name], for my lawful wife, to have and to hold, from this day forward, for better, for worse, for richer, for poorer, in sickness and in health, until death do us part.

I, [name], take you, [name], for my lawful husband, to have and to hold, from this day forward, for better, for worse, for richer, for poorer, in sickness and in health, until death do us part.

Hindu

Considering the diversity of marriage practices in the Hindu traditions, there is no uniform wording followed by all groups. The complex wedding ceremony, or Vivaaha, is based on the marriage of Soma and Surya in the Vedas (sacred texts). No Western-style vows are exchanged. Instead, the bride and groom perform the rite of Saptapadi, where they physically take seven steps together as they make seven promises that relate to marriage commitment and symbolize the journey through life. The Seven Steps may be stated or can be physically or symbolically represented, but the rite is always performed around the nuptial fire of the deity Agni, the Radiant One.

With God as our guide, let us take:
the first step to nourish each other
the second step to grow together in strength
the third step to preserve our wealth
the fourth step to share our joys and sorrows
the fifth step to care for our children
the sixth step to be together forever
the seventh step to remain lifelong friends,
the perfect halves to make a perfect whole.

Islam

Muslim marriage consists of two parts, the nikah and the walima. The nikah is the binding of the couple in a legal ceremony while the walima is the celebration in honor of the union. During the nikah, an imam (religious leader) speaks about marriage, and verses from the Koran, or Quran, are read; most couples do not exchange vows, but some do say something along the lines of the following:

I, [bride's name], offer you myself in marriage in accordance with the instructions of the Holy Quran and the Holy Prophet, peace and blessing be upon Him. I pledge, in honesty and with sincerity, to be for you an obedient and faithful wife.

I pledge, in honesty and sincerity, to be for you a faithful and helpful husband.

Judaism

The different branches of Judaism offer some variations in the wedding ceremony, and indeed each synagogue and rabbi may have their own interpretation. While the exchange of spoken vows is not part of a traditional Jewish ceremony, they have now been incorporated into some Reform and Conservative ceremonies as more couples wish to make a verbal pledge to one another. Again, be sure to check with your own rabbi to determine your synagogue's accepted format.

REFORM

RABBI: And now I ask you, in the presence of God and this assembly: Do you, [name], take [name] to be your wife, to love, to honor, and to cherish? *I do.*

And do you, [name], take [name] to be your husband, to love, to honor, and to cherish? *I do.*

[Name] and [name], speak the words and exchange the rings that make you husband and wife. [Name], as you place the ring on the finger of the one you love, recite the words that formally unite you in marriage.

Couples then answer the rabbi with one of the options below:

Option I
GROOM: Be consecrated to me with this ring as my wife in keeping with the heritage of Moses and Israel.

BRIDE: Be consecrated to me with this ring as my husband in keeping with the heritage of Moses and Israel.

Option II
GROOM: Be wedded to me with this ring as my wife in keeping with the religion of the Jewish People.

BRIDE: Be wedded to me with this ring as my wife in keeping with the religion of the Jewish People.

CONSERVATIVE

GROOM: By this ring, you are consecrated to me, as my wife, in accordance with the laws of Moses and the people of Israel.

BRIDE: I am my beloved's and my beloved is mine.

~~~~~~~~
ORTHODOX
~~~~~~~~

Only the groom states an ancient Aramaic vow when placing a ring on his bride's finger:

Behold thou are consecrated unto me with this ring according to the law of Moses and of Israel.

The Seven Blessings, or Sheva Berachot, are part of any Jewish wedding ceremony and are said after the vows. There are many different versions; this one is taken from a conservative rabbi manual:

Praised are You, God, who brings forth fruit from the vine.

Praised are You, God, who shapes the universe. All things created speak of Your glory.

Praised are You, Holy One, who fashions each person.

We praise You, God, for forming each person in Your image. You have planted within us a vision of You and given us the means that we may flourish through time. Praised are You, creator of humanity.

May Israel, once bereft of her children, now delight as

they gather together in joy. Praised are You, God, who lets Zion rejoice with her children.

Let these loving friends taste of the bliss You gave to the first man and woman in the Garden of Eden in the days of old. Praised are You, the Presence who dwells with the bride and groom in delight.

Praised are You, who lights the world with happiness and contentment, love and companionship, peace and friendship, bridegroom and bride. Let the mountains of Israel dance! Let the gates of Jerusalem ring with the sounds of joy, song, merriment, and delight—the voice of the groom and the voice of the bride, the happy shouts of their friends and companions. We praise You, God, who brings bride and groom together to rejoice in each other.

~~~~~~

Shinto

Traditionally there are no spoken vows in a Shinto wedding. However, during the San-San-Kudo, or Sake Ceremony, of the wedding, the bride and groom perform silent vows by taking three sips of sake from each of three different sized cups in three rounds together. These three rounds symbolize giving thanks to their ancestors, a promise to be together as long as they live, and a prayer for a happy home and chil-

dren. After the San-San-Kudo is complete, some couples may
make a statement along the lines of the following:

On this auspicious day, a wedding ceremony was performed in front of the kami. From this day forward, we will love each other, respect each other, share our sorrows and challenges, express appreciation to our ancestors, and continue to perpetuate the lineage. We humbly ask for your eternal protection.

Sikh

In the elaborate Anand Karaj (ceremony of bliss), the Sikh
bride and groom perform silent vows as they circle the holy
book, the Guru Granth Sahib, clockwise after each of four
different readings. Known as lavans, these four verses
explain the four stages of love and married life. The first
verse emphasizes the performance of duty to the family and
the community. The second verse is about yearning and love
for each other. The third verse refers to the stage of detach-
ment. The fourth verse refers to the final stage of harmony
and union in married life during which human love blends
into the love for God. These four lavans are from the Guru
Ram Das:

The First Lavan

In the first round of the marriage ceremony, the Lord sets out His Instructions for performing the daily duties of married life.

Instead of the hymns of the Vedas to Brahma, embrace the righteous conduct of Dharma, and renounce sinful actions.

Meditate on the Lord's Name; embrace and enshrine the contemplative remembrance of the Naam.

Worship and adore the Guru, the Perfect True Guru, and all your sinful residues shall be dispelled.

By great good fortune, celestial bliss is attained, and the Lord, Har Har, seems sweet to the mind.

Servant Nanak proclaims that, in this, the first round of the marriage ceremony, the marriage ceremony has begun.

The Second Lavan

In the second round of the marriage ceremony, the Lord leads you to meet the True Guru, the Primal Being.

With the Fear of God, the Fearless Lord in the mind, the filth of egotism is eradicated.

In the Fear of God, the Immaculate Lord, sing the Glorious Praises of the Lord, and behold the Lord's Presence before you.

The Lord, the Supreme Soul, is the Lord and Master of the Universe; He is pervading and permeating everywhere, fully filling all spaces.

Deep within, and outside as well, there is only the One Lord God.

Meeting together, the humble servants of the Lord sing the songs of joy.

Servant Nanak proclaims that, in this, the second round of the marriage ceremony, the unstruck sound current of the Shabad resounds.

The Third Lavan

In the third round of the marriage ceremony, the mind is filled with Divine Love.

Meeting with the humble Saints of the Lord, I have found the Lord, by great good fortune.

I have found the Immaculate Lord, and I sing the Glorious Praises of the Lord.

I speak the Word of the Lord's Bani.

By great good fortune, I have found the humble Saints, and I speak the Unspoken Speech of the Lord.

The Name of the Lord, Har Har, vibrates and resounds within my heart; meditating on the Lord, I have realized the destiny inscribed upon my forehead.

Servant Nanak proclaims that, in this, the third round of the marriage ceremony, the mind is filled with Divine Love for the Lord.

The Fourth Lavan

In the fourth round of the marriage ceremony, my mind has become peaceful; I have found the Lord.

As Gurmukh, I have met Him, with intuitive ease; the Lord seems so sweet to my mind and body.

The Lord seems so sweet; I am pleasing to my God.

Night and day, I lovingly focus my consciousness on the Lord.

I have obtained my Lord and Master, the fruit of my mind's desires.

The Lord's Name resounds and resonates.

The Lord God, my Lord and Master, blends with His bride, and her heart blossoms forth in the Naam.

Servant Nanak proclaims that, in this, the fourth round of the marriage ceremony, we have found the Eternal Lord God.

Unitarian/Universalist

[Name], will you take [name] to be your wife; love, honor, and cherish her now and forevermore? *I will.*

[Name], will you take [name] to be your husband; love, honor, and cherish him now and forevermore? *I will.*

I, [name], take you, [name], to be my wife; to have and to hold from this day forward, for better for worse, for richer, for poorer, in sickness and in health, to love and cherish always.

I, [name], take you, [name], to be my husband; to have and to hold from this day forward, for better for worse, for richer, for poorer, in sickness and in health, to love and cherish always.

[Name], will you have [name] to be your wife, to live together in creating and abiding marriage? Will you love and honor, comfort and cherish her in sickness and in health, in sorrow and in joy, from this day forward? *I will.*

[Name], will you have [name] to be your husband, to live together in creating and abiding marriage? Will you love and honor, comfort and cherish her in sickness and in health, in sorrow and in joy, from this day forward? *I will.*

Non-Religious Spiritual Vows

Wedding vows do not always have to be professed in a church or temple to feel spiritual. A couple seeking vows with a sense of gravitas or sacredness might look to the words of non-religious philosophy or various cultural texts held dear by generations as their vow inspiration.

HUMANIST PHILOSOPHY

According to the American Humanist Association, humanism is "a progressive life stance that, without supernaturalism, affirms our ability and responsibility to lead meaningful, ethical lives capable of adding to the greater good of humanity." Vows from humanist wedding ceremonies stress the mutuality between partners and equality among the sexes. Because such vows have their base in nonsectarian philosophy, they may be appropriate for those without a traditional religious affiliation. Here are two versions.

Version I

I acknowledge my love and respect for you and invite you to share my life as I hope to share yours. I promise always to recognize you as an equal individual and always to be conscious of your development as well as my own. I shall seek through kindness and understanding to achieve with you the life we have envisioned.

Version II

I, [name], promise you, [name], that I will be your
[wife/husband] from this day forward,
to be faithful and honest in every way,
to honor the faith and trust you place in me,
to love and respect you in your successes and in your
    failures,
to make you laugh and to be there when you cry,
to care for you in sickness and in health,
to softly kiss you when you are hurting,
and to be your companion and your friend, on this
    journey that we make together.

THE NATIVE AMERICAN SPIRIT

The poetic words of Native American prayers and songs are moving and inspiring in the context of creating vows for a wedding ceremony.

Apache Wedding Prayer

Now you will feel no rain,
For each of you will be shelter to the other.
Now you will feel no cold,
For each of you will be warmth to the other.
Now there is no more loneliness,
For each of you will be companion to the other.
Now you are two bodies,
But there is only one life before you.
Go now to your dwelling place
To enter into the days of your togetherness
And may your days be good and long upon the earth.

Eskimo Love Song

You are my husband/wife.
My feet shall run because of you.
My feet dance because of you.
My heart shall beat because of you.
My eyes see because of you.
My mind thinks because of you.
And I shall love because of you.

Iroquois Tribal Wish

May you have a safe tent
And no sorrow as you travel.

May happiness attend you in all your paths.
May you keep a heart like the morning,
And may you come slow to the four corners
Where man says goodnight.

Navajo Wedding Prayer

Now you have lit a fire and that fire should not go out. The two of you now have a fire that represents love, understanding, and a philosophy of life. It will give you heat, food, warmth, and happiness. The new fire represents a new beginning—a new life and a new family. The fire should keep burning; you should stay together. You have lit the fire for life, until old age separates you.

Shoshone Love Poem

Fair is the white star of twilight, and the sky clearer at
 the day's end;
But she is fairer, and she is dearer,
She, my heart's friend.

Fair is the white star of twilight, and the moon roving
 to the sky's end;
But she is fairer, better worth loving,
She, my heart's friend.

Regardless of their religious affiliation, some African-American couples choose to incorporate the slave tradition of "jumping the broom" into their wedding ceremony. A broom is placed on the floor and the couple jumps over it as part of their vows. The following traditional poem is sometimes read.

Dark and stormy may come the weather,
This man and woman are joined together.
Let none but him that makes the thunder,
Put this man and woman asunder.
I therefore announce you both the same,
Be good, go long, and keep up your name.
The broomstick's jumped, the world's not wide,
She's now your own, go kiss your bride!

Love is life.
All, everthing that I understand,
    I understand only because I love.
        Everything is, everything exists, only because I love.

— LEO TOLSTOY

CHAPTER THREE

WRITING YOUR OWN VOWS

PRE-EXISTING WEDDING VOWS have their merits, but there is something undeniably heartfelt and real about pledging vows that have sprung from your own minds and hands. After all, who can better convey the terms of your commitment than the two of you? Vows you have written yourself reflect the very unique love you share.

Personal vows can stand on their own or be used to supplement religious or civil vows. Though some houses of worship may not allow vows other than those in their own prayer books, personally-penned vows can be appropriate for many different ceremonies and couples. For example, brides and grooms who are planning an interfaith ceremony can write their own vows to accommodate both sets of beliefs. Those who do not wish to use words associated with a particular faith can write their own non-denominational vows, while others who desire to inject some feeling into their civil ceremonies might pen a few words to say after their government-issue vows. And for couples who strive to truly personalize every aspect of their wedding, handcrafted vows are the only way to go.

Whatever the driving force is behind writing your own vows, perhaps the most important reason is how the exercise really compels you to reflect upon the commitment you are about to make. Your ceremony will take on a new meaning because you took an active role and made a direct contribution.

First Things First

There are two initial conversations that should transpire prior to even considering writing your own vows. The first, of course, is with your partner. Perhaps this goes without saying, but creating your own vows is a dual effort. It's kind of like ordering a tasting menu at a restaurant—both of you have to be on board to take part. You may divvy up other wedding planning responsibilities, such as choosing the flowers or planning the honeymoon, but vow writing is a meaningful and important collaboration—not just for your wedding day, but for your relationship overall. Crucial, too, is that both of you are not only partners in this project, but equally willing partners—strong-arming your future spouse into participating in this endeavor could have disastrous results, and, frankly, goes against the concept as a whole. The second conversation you must have is with your officiant, as you'll need to determine any restrictions and lay down a few ground rules and establish some goals.

CLEAR THE CONCEPT WITH YOUR PARTNER

The two of you can decide whether or not you wish to write your own vows when you talk about the type of ceremony you envision—one that is in accordance with your shared religious tradition, one that combines your faiths in a respectful and contemporary way, one that is spiritual without being religious, or one that is purely secular. This will set the tone for the vows you create. Next come a few logistics. Decide if you will work on your vows independently or together. You'll have to choose a format for your vows, and consider whether you'll make individual or joint statements (see Chapter One for more on format). Some of these decisions will begin to flow and make more sense once you start your dialogue about your relationship. As a united front, aim to write vows of approximately the same length; most vows last no more than three minutes, which is much longer than you might think.

You should also plan on establishing a review policy for each other—will you work on drafts together or commit to secrecy until revealing your words of love at the ceremony? There are pros and cons to both methods. Reviewing one another's vows could prevent overlap of language or even something embarrassing for one of you from being said in front of family and friends. In collaboration you may work together or apart, reading your drafts to one another and working on revisions as a team, or simply passing your written version to your partner for his or her blessing. Admittedly, so much back and forth might take some of the magic away from when you actually will speak your vows. Hearing your partner proclaim his or her vow for the first time at the ceremony can be an exhilarating experience, but you also might be so nervous about what it is you are going to say that you might not really hear what it is that is being pledged to you. It's really a matter of what you're most comfortable with.

Lastly, set up a timeline and stick to it. Writing your wedding vows can be as short or long of a process as you wish to make it, but be realistic about having the time and energy to do it right. On the whole, you should allow about two months to prepare your vows and complete them no less than three days prior to the wedding. Remember that everyone's working style is different; be mindful of your partner's strengths—and weaknesses—when it comes to procrastinating, deadlines, and badgering.

CLEAR THE CONCEPT WITH YOUR OFFICIANT

Once you and your partner agree to write your own wedding-day pledges, make an appointment to talk things over with your officiant. If you plan on having your ceremony in a church or temple, you'll need to know whether your faith even allows vows that deviate from the norm. Your officiant will be aware of any guidelines for your particular house of worship, and can offer advice about matters such as length or suggestions of words, readings, or quotes. Also, talk to your officiant about the exact point where the vows will occur in your ceremony (see page xiii for common placement), and what it is that he or she might plan to say as well. It is also important to establish how the vows are to be delivered—in public or private, with or without a microphone, with first names or full names—and if your officiant will help you remember what it is you wrote if need be. If you know your officiant well

DO be distinctive. If you're making the effort to write your own vows, they should be unique to your relationship. Cite specific instances in your lives, and avoid broad turns of phrase and cliches that could apply to anyone.

DON'T make your public pronouncement for insiders only. It's okay to mention personal moments, but make sure everyone can understand them. After all, your vows are a public declaration of your commitment, so your witnesses should be able to understand them.

DO infuse your vows with your personality, but use humor with a light hand. Remember the commitment you are making is a serious one, and consider the setting in which you are making your vows. For example, an oft-quoted celebrity vow to "always make your favorite banana shake" would seem out of place in a ceremony at a formal cathedral or temple, but might be apropos following a basic civil ceremony or a ceremony in a more casual location such as a restaurant or garden.

DON'T reveal anything too intimate. While your vows are a public statement about your relationship, certain aspects—sexual matters or how you stole your partner from your best friend—are probably best kept private.

DO sound like yourself. Even though you wish to sound polished, avoid getting so wrapped up in referencing the Romantic poets that you try and imitate them in your speech patterns.

DON'T repeat yourself. Be on the lookout for words that appear over and over. If you need to, delete some instances or consult a thesaurus to make every word count and stand on its own.

DO keep it short and sweet. A vow is a declaration, not a dissertation. Use concise sentences; vows that are to the point are often the most powerful.

DON'T use negative language. For example, "I'll always be by your side" is preferable to "I'll never leave you."

DO address your future spouse by name. Not only are you making an on-the-record statement of whom you are marrying, but you are also giving your beloved the opportunity to hear the sound of his or her own name rolling off your tongue.

and value his or her opinion, you might wish to include him or her in a round or two of drafts for commentary, but at the very least be sure to provide him or her with a copy of your vows once they are finished.

REFLECTION AND DISCUSSION

Now we've come to the fun part—exploring exactly what it is that makes you such a perfect match. To get your creative juices flowing, the first part of the exercise requires taking some time to reflect on your own feelings about your partner, yourself, and what marriage means to you. Once you feel like you know where you stand, plan on getting your heads—and hearts— together for a romantic discussion about the state of your union. In the midst of catering menu tastings, gown fittings, and all the other parts often involved in planning a modern-day wedding, this task is undoubtedly a welcome respite and will help you both focus on the true meaning of your wedding day. Think of this discussion as not only what you want your wedding vows to be, but also what you wish your marriage to be like. Chances are that talking about your relationship will reaffirm what you already know and love about each other and why you wish to publicly seal your union. At the very most, you may uncover important issues you may need to discuss prior to exchanging your official vows. Be honest and true to yourself and each other.

LOOKING INSIDE YOURSELF

You can prepare for your discussion with your partner with a little introspection. Take an hour or so, maybe over a cup of coffee or in a quiet corner of your home, to simply think and reflect. Ponder the meanings the following words have for you, and jot down your thoughts in a notebook or journal:

Love
Marriage
Partner
Fidelity
Commitment
Promise
Trust
Family
Future

Next, write down ten words or phrases that describe your partner and ten that describe your relationship. You don't need to agonize over this—it's really just to get you thinking. Some of the language or sentiments

you record may be the seeds for what you will ultimately say in your vow.

This next assignment involves a series of questions to
ask each other and yourself. There are a couple of different ways you can approach this. You can answer and
discuss the questions together, answer them independently as part of your self-reflection above and then discuss your answers together, or answer them independently and exchange your answers to read alone and then
come together to discuss the tact you will take. Whatever your method, take lots of notes and try to find
common threads of thought from which you might be
able to extract themes for your vows.

Mark a day on the calendar for your discussion and
make a date of it. It is important to be in the right
frame of mind. You should feel relaxed and loving; don't
plan to get together during a time when you'll be
stressed out from work, and if you've just had a wed-
ding-planning-fueled argument, by all means resched-
ule. Also, elect to meet in an environment conducive to
the task at hand—somewhere quiet and private, where
there are few distractions and you both feel comfortable and free to talk about your thoughts and feelings.
A shared apartment where your roommate is popping

in and out or a busy restaurant might not be the best locations. The nature of this discussion can make your emotions surge, so be sure to have a box of tissues nearby. One more thing: Turn off the technology and impose a television-, cellphone-, and email-free working zone to help you focus on each other. The rest of the world can wait!

PART ONE — REVIEW YOUR HISTORY
Begin by recalling the important events and turning points of your relationship.

- When and where did you meet?
- What did you initially like about one another when you first met? What do you like about one another now?
- When did you know you loved this person? When did you tell him or her?
- How and when did you know he or she was "the one"?
- Are there any meaningful episodes or obstacles you've overcome together? How did you deal with them? How did you feel about each other afterward?
- What are some of your favorite memories of times together? Why are these important?

If writer's block afflicts you, take a moment to review this list of words for inspiration. Think about how they may apply to you, your partner, and your relationship as a whole, and perhaps use a few as a starting point for your declaration of love.

Absolute	Challenges	Declare
Adore	Cherish	Deserving
Adventure	Comfort	Devotion
Affection	Committed	Dignity
Always	Communication	Dream
Appreciate	Companion	Encourage
Aspirations	Compassion	Enduring
Beginning	Complement	Entrust
Beloved	Complete	Eternal
Blessed	Confidante	Eternity
Bond	Connect	Experience
Camaraderie	Connection	Faithful
Care	Constant	Fidelity
Celebrate	Cooperation	Forever
	Covenant	
	Dear	

Friend	Meaning	Side by side
Friendship	Mindful	Soul
Fulfilled	Mutual	Soul mate
Future	Nurture	Steadfast
Gift	One	Strengthen
Goals	Partner	Support
Grow	Patient	Thankful
Happiness	Pledge	Together
Harmony	Possibilities	Treasure
Heart	Precious	True
Honest	Promise	Trust
Honor	Pure	Unconditional
Hope	Real	Understanding
Ideal	Regard	Union
Inspiration	Relationship	Unite
Integrity	Respect	Unity
Join	Responsible	Unwavering
Journey	Sacred	Uphold
Joy	Search	Value
Learning	Share	Wish
Lifetime		Worthy
Loyal		

These phrases are timeless and meaningful for expressing
your thoughts about the following subjects.

Time	All the days of my life
	As long as we both shall live
	From this day forward
	All of our days
Emotion	From the depths of my heart
	Hand in hand, heart to heart
	With all my heart
You/I	I give myself to you
	Make/spend our lives together
	By my/your side
	Partner in life
	All that I am
	You above all others
	Hearts/souls as one
	My destined mate
	Your days are mine, as mine are yours
Pledge	This is my solemn vow
	Without reservation

Next, examine who you are, as individuals and as a couple.

- What do you love about your partner?
- What qualities do you admire in this person?
- What qualities does your partner elicit from you?
- What are your similarities? What are your differences?
- How does it feel to be in love with this person?
- What are the fundamental reasons you are together? Why are you better as a couple than apart?
- Are there meaningful words—song lyrics, a poem, a religious passage—that have resonance for your relationship?

PART THREE — REFLECT ON THE IDEA OF MARRIAGE

You've decided to marry; explore your thoughts behind your decision.

- When did you decide to get married? Why?
- What does marriage mean to you?
- What makes a successful marriage?
- What do you hope to be able to give in your marriage? What do you feel you need from your marriage?
- Discuss the marriages of people who are close to

you: your parents, your future in-laws, your grand-parents, close family friends—what is it that you admire about their unions? What can you learn from them?

PART FOUR — *IDENTIFY GOALS AND PROMISES*
Outline the path of your future as your lives progress.

- What do you want to achieve as a couple?
- How do you envision growing old together? What do you hope the future may bring as your lives unfold?
- What future challenges might come your way?
- What promises do you wish to make?

Inspiring Words

All your life, you've probably been taught not to plagiarize someone else's work. Generally, this is good advice with regards to term papers, screenplays, magazine assignments, and the like. But when it comes to creating your wedding vows, feel free to borrow words, phrases, or ideas from existing material if they mean something to you and your love for your future spouse and can usefully supplement the thoughts you collected in your heart-to-heart discussion. The following are all good references for scribing your vows.

As mentioned before, the traditional religious wedding vows and prayers as found in Chapter Two can be excerpted or adapted to meet your needs. If you like, consult texts and teachings such as the Bible, Koran, Torah, Tao Te Ching, or the Confucian Analects, etc. All offer spiritual guidance and universal words of wisdom, regardless of your own religious or non-religious background.

SECULAR RESOURCES

Themes of love and devotion have sparked some of the greatest works of literature and verses of poetry, so why not consult these writings to fuel your own words of passion and promise? Many appropriate selections can be found in Chapter Five, but if you have a favorite author or poet be sure to consider his or her work as well. And don't stop at writings geared toward adults—some children's books contain ideas that could translate into words for wedding vows (see page 58 for a list of suggestions). If you prefer fact to fiction, you might look into the world's most famous love stories and love letters for inspiration. Cultural influences, such as lines from classic movies or lyrics from popular songs, might have just the words for what you are trying to say.

When penning your own words of promise, why not consider the sentiments expressed in letters written by famous lovers? You may not agree with their philosophies or politics, but you can't fault the power of their passion. You'll find a few excerpts in Chapter Five, but may also want to look up the letters from:

John Keats and Fanny Brawne
Ronald and Nancy Reagan
William Butler Yeats and Maud Gonne
Simone de Beauvoir and Jean Paul Sartre
F. Scott and Zelda Fitzgerald
The Duke and Duchess of Windsor
Leonard and Virginia Woolf
Winston and Clementine Churchill
Elizabeth Barrett and Robert Browning

In a similar way to poetry, song lyrics—really a form of poetry themselves—can convey a depth of feeling about love for another person. You can use songs to simply get in the mood while crafting your own vows, or you might even "borrow" a phrase or two from meaningful lyrics. Have a listen to the songs of these lyricists, composers, musicians, and singers.

LEGENDS: The Beach Boys, The Beatles, Elvis Presley

CLASSIC CROONERS: Nat King Cole, Harry Connick Jr., Bobby Darin, Dean Martin, Frank Sinatra

CONTEMPORARY SONGSTRESSES: Dido, Norah Jones, Sarah McLaughlin, Joni Mitchell

DYNAMIC SONGWRITING DUOS: Gilbert and Sullivan, Kander and Ebb, Leiber and Stoller, Rodgers and Hammerstein, Rodgers and Hart

SULTRY CHANTEUSES: Ella Fitzgerald, Billie Holiday, Etta James, Sarah Vaughn

MEN AND WOMEN OF MOTOWN: Marvin Gaye, The Four Tops, The Temptations, The Supremes, Stevie Wonder

WITTY WORDSMITHS: Noel Coward, Cole Porter

Sometimes, the simplicity of the language in children's literature says it all. Look back fondly on some favorites from your younger years for words to express your love.

Guess How Much I Love You—Sam McBratney
The Little Prince—Antoine de Saint-Exupery
The Owl and The Pussycat—Edward Lear
The Steadfast Tin Soldier—Hans Christian Andersen
Tom Sawyer—Mark Twain
The Velveteen Rabbit—Margery Williams
Winnie the Pooh—A.A. Milne

A few words of caution: If you are borrowing from an older work or use language from vows of past generations, you may wish to update any antiquated language like "man and wife" to "husband and wife" or strive to make sure there is a balance of equality. And, if you do choose words from a spiritual text or secular work, be sure you thoroughly understand what they mean. Furthermore, if you have selected a quote or excerpt be aware of the overall message of the complete work; while something might sound great out of context, you might realize the reference is not appropriate. For example, the narrator of Edgar Allan Poe's *Annabel Lee* claims that, "we loved with a love that was more than love;" it's a great ode to the power of love, but sadly the lady he speaks of now lies buried in a sepulcher by the sea, which is not exactly the type of image you want to invoke at your wedding.

PERSONAL RESOURCES

While you may feel that the writings of the great prophets and philosophers are a tough act to follow, don't overlook your own ability to express your emotions. Look back on pieces of your own correspondence to one another—letters, cards, notes, faxes, and emails and even journal entries, drawings, and photographs—to be inspired by moments in your relation-

❧ INCLUDING CHILDREN

Oftentimes, if a person is marrying someone with children from a previous marriage or relationship, it is a meaningful gesture to not only make a vow to the parent, but also to the child as well to acknowledge the new family formed by the couple's union. A vow might mention a child by name, or perhaps even provide some words for the child to speak him- or herself. If you would like to do something along these lines, be sure to involve the child from the beginning and gently discuss what he or she would be comfortable saying or doing.

ship when you felt a certain way about your partner. If you have been moved by weddings of friends and family, ask the couple if they would be willing to share their vows and readings with you.

Putting Pen to Paper

At last the time has come to finally start the actual writing part of this process. To begin, gather all of your resources and inspirations, and the answers to your Q&A (see page 49). Set aside some time dedicated solely to this project; don't try to squeeze it in between other tasks like doing your laundry or making dinner.

Even though we live in a computerized society, try to write your vows by hand, using a nice pen and stationery or a good notebook as even your notes and drafts might be something you want to keep. Alternatively, if you are more comfortable speaking than writing, you may wish to initially record your thoughts into a tape recorder and transcribe them later. Whether you write or speak, it may take a few sessions over the course of days or weeks to thoroughly collect your thoughts. Don't worry if you think you are a terrible writer or don't have a way with words—you can make as many drafts and edits as you like until you are happy with your vows.

Start by jotting down some initial musings—key words, thoughts, or phrases, either from your own head or borrowed from one of your sources of inspiration. Their provenance doesn't matter so much as how they express what you feel. Remember, even though you are "writing your own vows" you don't have to completely reinvent the wheel—you can adapt bits of existing vows or writing to fit your thoughts. You might wish to make a list of all the things that are important to you with regards to your partner and to marriage as a concept.

Write from the heart—how you really feel. Nothing is too sappy. Let your emotions flow and don't be afraid of soul-baring language. At this stage, don't worry about length or grammar; just get your point across first, and you can edit out things that don't work later.

YOUR SECOND DRAFT

Now consider the style of vow you and your partner have chosen, and start to work some of your thoughts and phrases into that format. Also try to incorporate language that gives your vows a personal flavor. Is there something you can draw upon from your relationship or who you are? For example, if you are both musicians you can borrow language from your shared passion, and speak of your "harmony" or the "music of your hearts." If you carried on a long-distance relationship, you might add in something about how your relationship blossomed despite the miles and time differences, or how sheer geography alone wouldn't keep you from being together. If need be, carry on to a third or fourth draft (or however many you need) until you feel you comfortable with what you have—then it's time for editing.

EDIT AND REVISE

Once you feel you have something close to a final draft, it's time to edit and make any last revisions. Be sure you stand behind every statement one hundred percent and cross out any words or phrases that don't work. Reread the sentences and phrases you feel the most strongly about—be aware of which parts might make you laugh or cry. Experiment with order and move sentences or whole sections around until you have the most natural flow. Consider your use of language—the tone and vocabulary should be authentic to who you are, and to the nature of your relationship. Lastly, if you have chosen to make your personal vows in tandem with religious vows, review the two closely to make sure there are no repetitive words or themes. See page 44 for some other dos and don'ts to remember.

Ready to shout it from the rooftops? Hold on, there is one additional step. Read your final draft out loud in the presence of someone else—either your future spouse if you have agreed to share your vows before the ceremony, or a trusted friend with a good ear who will give you an honest critique. Make any last adjustments, then read your vow aloud again and time yourself. If you are running long, pare down your vow phrase by phrase and keep your best material. Congratulations! You did it.

Love many things, for therein lies the true strength,
and whatsoever loves much performs much,
and can accomplish much,
and what is done in love is well done.

—VINCENT VAN GOGH

CHAPTER FOUR

SAYING YOUR PIECE

IF YOU'RE NOT ACCUSTOMED to public speaking, the thought of saying something in front of a crowd might be a little nerve-racking. And if that something is your public profession of your love and commitment to your soon-to-be husband or wife, you might be positively terrified. Regardless of whether you are repeating cherished vows spoken by brides and grooms throughout history or reciting vows you wrote yourself, it's perfectly natural to feel a little anxious as your wedding day approaches. Never fear—you can pledge your vows with grace and confidence with these practical pointers in mind.

Preparation

One of the most oft-repeated public-speaking tips is to know your material. Read through your vow carefully, and make a mental note of potential stumbling blocks like tricky alliteration, extra-long sentences, and emotion-charged words or phrases. If there are things you still wish to fix, do so now (this is your last opportunity to tinker with your vows). Otherwise, if you know your demons, you can embrace them—or at least brace yourself for them when you see them coming! Identify natural places to pause for emphasis or to catch your breath. Even if you think you'd like to memorize your vow, print or type out the words on index cards—the wedding-day mind works in mysterious ways, and you wouldn't want to just be standing there with nothing to say if your mind goes blank. People get nervous, cards get lost, so have a backup plan in place. Ask one of your attendants to carry your vow cards for you on the day of the ceremony, and also give a final copy to your officiant a couple of days prior. You may also wish to write out your vow on a pretty piece of paper as a memento (see more keepsake ideas on page 71).

Practice

An actor wouldn't dream of stepping onstage without having rehearsed his or her lines, and neither should you. Read your vow out loud, when you are alone. Listen to your own voice. Practice speaking slowly, but naturally, and say each word clearly. The goal is to sound confident that you believe in what you are saying. Experiment with different inflections or change the emphasis on certain words. Also, try to read your vow in front of a mirror so you can see the shift in your expressions. Visualize yourself saying your vow to your partner.

Then, rehearse your vow with your partner (if you're not waiting to reveal your vows at the ceremony) to see how your vows work in tandem or with a trusted friend for an honest critique of your delivery.

Take full advantage of any ceremony rehearsals scheduled. Assess the space where your wedding will take place, and test the loudness of your voice within it. If you will be using a microphone on the big day, be sure you know how to operate it and practice saying something with the actual device in place (though you probably don't want to say your real vows so as not to spoil the magic of your actual ceremony).

Day of Delivery

The day has come. Breathe deeply, and you're ready to begin. Everyone is cheering you on! Take your time and speak slowly and clearly—just like you practiced. Use as strong a voice as you can muster so friends and family all the way to the back of the room can hear you. Look deep into your partner's eyes as you say your names and your promises—it's an unforgettable experience.

Know that you won't be the first bride or groom whose voice wavered with emotion or who has even made mistakes. If you mess up your words, simply carry on where you left off. Chances are, it is only you who noticed. It might comfort you to know that in one of the most widely watched wedding ceremonies of all time, Lady Diana Spencer scrambled the series of Prince Charles' names—in essence marrying "Philip Charles Arthur George" instead of "Charles Philip Arthur George." If you start to cry, don't try to speak if you can't; take a deep breath, and continue once you've regained your composure. There's no need for apologies—it is more than likely yours will not be the only teary eyes in the house.

And when your partner recites his or her vow, listen closely to the words so you can hold this amazing experience in your memory forever. It is a moment you have thought about, discussed, and worked toward, but now is the time to enjoy it, and feel it. You have committed yourselves to one another. Congratulations—you are married!

✎ WORDS FOR POSTERITY

If you have written your own vows, or are exchanging vows in a foreign language or complex ceremony, you may wish to print the words in your ceremony program or make photocopies to distribute to guests. This is also helpful if the ceremony space is large and your family and friends will have a hard time hearing you. As a keepsake, you could frame a beautifully handwritten or calligraphed version of your vows or include a copy in your wedding photo album or scrapbook. You may even wish to renew your vows on your anniversary every year.

Love is, above all else, the gift of oneself.

—JEAN ANOUILH

CHAPTER FIVE

WORDS TO INSPIRE

THE FOLLOWING is a select group of quotes, poetry, and assorted writings with themes related to love and marriage. Their purpose here is to inspire—feel free to incorporate any of these words or their sentiments into your wedding vows. If you are not writing your own vows, you might wish to share these works with your partner or use them to personalize printed materials like your programs or invitations. You may have some of your own favorite works of literature and poetry to add to their ranks, but as mentioned before if you intend to use such words for your wedding ceremony just make sure the overall meaning they have and the context they are from are appropriate to the occasion.

Love and the Heart

It is only with the heart that one can see rightly, what is essential is invisible to the eye.

—ANTOINE DE SAINT-EXUPÉRY

The best and most beautiful things in the world cannot be seen or even touched. They must be felt with the heart.

—HELEN KELLER

A loving heart is the truest wisdom.

—CHARLES DICKENS

Love does not consist of gazing at each other,
but looking outward in the same direction.

—ANTOINE DE SAINT-EXUPÉRY

From *Les Miserables*
VICTOR HUGO

The greatest happiness of life is the conviction that we are loved, loved for ourselves, or rather loved in spite of ourselves.

At the touch of love, everyone becomes a poet.

—PLATO

To love and be loved is to feel the sun from both sides.

—DAVID VISCOTT

Love has nothing to do with what you are expecting to get only with what you are expecting to give—which is everything.

—KATHARINE HEPBURN

Love is what you've been through with somebody.

—JAMES THURBER

To love is to be vulnerable.

—C.S. LEWIS

There is only one happiness in life, to love and be loved.

—GEORGE SAND

Our truest life is when we are in dreams awake.

—HENRY DAVID THOREAU

To love is to find pleasure in the happiness of the person loved.

—LEIBNITZ

Love is composed of a single soul inhabiting two bodies.

—ARISTOTLE

Sonnet XVII

PABLO NERUDA

Translated by Stephen Mitchell

I don't love you as if you were the salt-rose, topaz
or arrow of carnations that propagate fire:
I love you as certain dark things are loved,
secretly, between the shadow and the soul.

I love you as the plant that doesn't bloom and carries
hidden within itself the light of those flowers,
and thanks to your love, darkly in my body
lives the dense fragrance that rises from the earth.

I love you without knowing how, or when, or from
    where,
I love you simply, without problems or pride:
I love you in this way because I know no other way of
    loving

but this, in which there is no I or you,
so intimate that your hand upon my chest is my hand,
so intimate that when I fall asleep it is your eyes that
    close.

From *Sonnets from the Portuguese,* Sonnet XLIII

ELIZABETH BARRETT BROWNING

How do I love thee? Let me count the ways.
I love thee to the depth and breadth and height
My soul can reach, when feeling out of sight
For the ends of Being and ideal Grace.
I love thee to the level of everyday's
Most quiet need, by sun and candle-light.
I love thee freely, as men strive for Right;
I love thee purely, as they turn from Praise.
I love thee with the passion put to use
In my old griefs, and with my childhood's faith.
I love thee with a love I seemed to lose
With my lost saints, —I love thee with the breath,
Smiles, tears, of all my life! —and, if God choose,
I shall but love thee better after death.

From *The Prophet*

KAHLIL GIBRAN

Love has no other desire but to fulfill itself.
But if you love and must needs have desires, let these
    be your desires:
To melt and be like a running brook that sings its
    melody to the night.
To know the pain of too much tenderness.

To be wounded by your own understanding of love;
And to bleed willingly and joyfully.
To wake at dawn with a winged heart and give thanks
　　for another day of loving;
To rest at the noon hour and meditate love's ecstasy;
To return home at eventide with gratitude;
And then to sleep with a prayer for the beloved in your
　　heart
and a song of praise on your lips.

From *Know Thyself, Know Thyself More Deeply*
D.H. LAWRENCE

Go deeper than love, for the soul has greater depths,
love is like the grass, but the heart is deep wild rock
molten, yet dense and permanent.
Go down to your deep old heart, and lose sight of
　　yourself.
And lose sight of me, the me whom you turbulently
　　loved.
Let us lose sight of ourselves, and break the mirrors.
For the fierce curve of our lives is moving again to the
　　depths
out of sight, in the deep living heart.

From *Love Is Enough*
WILLIAM MORRIS

Love is enough; though the world be a-waning,
And the woods have no voice but the voice of
    complaining,
Though the sky be too dark for dim eyes to discover
The gold cups and daisies fair blooming thereunder,
Though the hills be held shadows, and the sea a dark
    wonder
And this day draw a veil over all deeds passed over,
Yet their hands shall not tremble, their feet shall not
    falter;
The void shall not weary, the fear shall not alter
Those lips and these eyes of the loved and the lover

From *Romeo and Juliet*
WILLIAM SHAKESPEARE

My bounty is as boundless as the sea,
My love as deep. The more I give to thee,
The more I have, for both are infinite.

From *Gift From The Sea*
ANNE MORROW LINDBERGH

When you love someone, you do not love them all the
time, in exactly the same way, from moment to mo-

ment. It is an impossibility. It is even a lie to pretend to. And yet this is exactly what most of us demand. We have so little faith in the ebb and flow of life, of love, of relationships. We leap at the flow of the tide and resist in terror its ebb. We are afraid it will never return. We insist on permanency, on duration, on continuity; when the only continuity possible, in life as in love, is in growth, in fluidity—in freedom in the sense that the dancers are free, barely touching as they pass, but partners in the same pattern.

Corinthians 13:1-13

If I speak in the tongues of men and of angels, but have not love, I am a noisy gong or a clanging cymbal. And if I have prophetic powers, and understand all mysteries and all knowledge, and if I have all faith, so as to remove mountains, but have not love, I am nothing. If I give away all I have, and if I deliver my body to be burned, but have not love, I gain nothing. Love is patient and kind; love is not jealous or boastful; it is not arrogant or rude. Love does not insist on its own way; it is not irritable or resentful; it does not rejoice at wrong, but rejoices in the right. Love bears all things, believes all things, hopes all things, endures all things. Love never ends; as for prophecies, they will pass away; as for tongues, they will cease; as for knowledge, it will pass away. For our knowledge is imperfect and our prophecy is imperfect; but when the perfect comes, the imperfect will pass away. When I was a child, I spoke like a child, I thought like a child, I reasoned like a child; when I became a man, I gave up childish ways. For now we see in a mirror dimly, but then face to face. Now I know in part; then I shall understand fully, even as I have been fully understood. So faith, hope, love abide, these three; but the greatest of these is love.

Oh, hasten not his loving act,
Rapture where self and not-self meet:
My life has been the awaiting you,
Your footfall was my own heart's beat.

— PAUL VALÉRY

The Good Morrow
JOHN DONNE

I wonder by my troth, what thou and I
Did, till we loved? were we not weaned till then?
But sucked on country pleasures, childishly?
Or snorted we i'the seven sleepers' den?
Twas so; But this, all pleasures fancies be.
If ever any beauty I did see,
Which I desired, and got, 'twas but a dream of thee.

And now good morrow to our waking souls,
Which watch not one another out of fear;
For love, all love of other sights controls,
And makes one little room, an everywhere.
Let sea-discoverers to new worlds have gone,
Let maps to others, worlds on worlds have shown,
Let us possess our world, each hath one, and is one.

My face in thine eye, thine in mine appears,
And true plain hearts do in the faces rest,
Where can we find two better hemispheres
Without sharp North, without declining West?
Whatever dies, was not mixed equally;
If our two loves be one, or, thou and I
Love so alike, that none do slacken, none can die.

The Presence of Love
SAMUEL TAYLOR COLERIDGE

And in Life's noisiest hour,
There whispers still the ceaseless Love of Thee,
The heart's Self-solace and soliloquy.
You mould my Hopes, you fashion me within;
And to the leading Love—throb in the Heart
Thro' all my Being, thro' my pulses beat;
You lie in all my many Thoughts, like Light,
Like the fair light of Dawn, or summer Eve

On rippling Stream, or cloud-reflecting Lake.
And looking to the heaven, that bends above you,
How oft! I bless the Lot, that made me love you.

From *Cyrano de Bergerac*
EDMOND ROSTAND

Cyrano speaking to Roxane, on behalf of Christian
"I love you, choke with love, I love you, dear...My brain
reels, I can bear no more, it is too much...Your name is
in my heart the golden clapper in a bell; and as I know
no rest, Roxane, always the heart is shaken, and ever
rings your name!"

A Red, Red Rose
ROBERT BURNS

O, my love is like a red, red rose,
That's newly sprung in June.
O my love is like the melody,
    That's sweetly played in tune.

As fair art thou, my bonnie lass,
    So deep in love am I,
And I will love thee still, my dear,
    Till a' the seas gang dry.

Till a' the seas gang dry, my dear,
    And the rocks melt wi' the sun!
And I will love thee still, my dear,
    While the sands o'life shall run.

And fare thee well, my only love,
    And fare thee well awhile!
And I will come again, my love,
    Though it were ten thousand mile!

A Birthday

CHRISTINA ROSSETTI

My heart is like a singing bird
    Whose nest is in a watered shoot;
My heart is like an apple-tree
Whose boughs are bent with thick-set fruit;
My heart is like a rainbow shell
    That paddles in a halcyon sea;
My heart is gladder than all these,
    Because my love is come to me.

Raise me a dais of silk and down;
    Hang it with vair and purple dyes;
Carve it in doves and pomegranates,
    And peacocks with a hundred eyes;

Work it in gold and silver grapes,
    In leaves and silver fleur-de-lys;
Because the birthday of my life
    Is come, my love has come to me.

My true love hath my heart, and I have his
SIR PHILIP SIDNEY

My true Love hath my heart, and I have his,
By just exchange one for the other given:
I hold his dear, and mine he cannot miss;
There never was a better bargain driven.
His heart in me keeps me and him in one,
My heart in him his thoughts and senses guides:
He loves my heart, for once it was his own;
I cherish his because in me it bides.
His heart his wound received from thy sight,
My heart was wounded with his wounded heart;
For as from me, on him his hurt did light,
So still methought in me his hurt did smart.
Both, equal hurt, in the is change sought our bliss:
My true love hath my heart, and I have his.

Love of You is Mixed Deep in My Vitals
AUTHOR UNKNOWN, Ancient Egyptian text
Translated by John L. Foster

Love of you is mixed deep in my vitals,
    Like water stirred into flour for bread,
Like simples compound in a sweet-tasting drug,
    Like pastry and honey mixed to perfection.

Oh, hurry to look at your love!
    Be like horses charging in battle,
Like a gardener up with the sun
    Burning to watch his prize bud open.

High heaven causes a girl's lovelonging.
    It is like being too far from the light,
Far from the hearth of familiar arms.
    It is this being so tangled in you.

Shall I Compare Thee to a Summer's Day
WILLIAM SHAKESPEARE

Shall I compare thee to a summer's day?
Thou art more lovely and more temperate:
Rough winds do shake the darling buds of May,
And summer's lease hath all too short a date:
Sometime too hot the eye of heaven shines,
And often is his gold complexion dimmed;

And every fair from fair sometime declines,
By chance,
Or nature's changing course untrimmed;
But thy eternal summer shall not fade,
Nor lose possession of that fair thou owest,
Nor shall Death brag thou wanderest in his shade,
When in eternal lines to time thou growest;
So long as men can breathe, or eyes can see,
So long lives this, and this gives life to thee.

Did I Ever Tell You

RICHARD EXLEY

Did I ever tell you
that I love you
early in the morning
with your toothpaste kisses
and your sleepy eyes?
With your headaches and
grumpiness
that only goes away
if I hold your hand
and whisper the soft things
you like to hear?

Did I ever tell you
that I love you

at mid-afternoon,
during coffee-break time,
when clocks and
crowded cafeterias
make smiles and warm hands
love's best language?
Did I ever tell you
that I love the way
you smell after a bath,
that I love the way you feel in bed beside me,
that I love the way
you look after I've loved you?

Did I ever tell you
that I love you?
I do,
I do,
I do.

The most wonderful of all things in life is the discovery of another human being with whom one's relationship has a growing depth, beauty and joy as the years increase. This inner progressiveness of love between two human beings is a most marvellous thing; it cannot be found by looking for it or by passionately wishing

for it. It is a sort of divine accident, and the most wonderful of all things in life.

—SIR HUGH WALPOLE

Love means to commit oneself without guarantee, to
give oneself completely in the hope that our love will
produce love in the loved person. Love is an act of faith,
and whoever is of little faith is also of little love.

—ERICH FROMM

Accept the things
To which fate binds you and
Love the people with whom fate
Brings you together
But do so with all your heart.

—MARCUS AURELIUS

True love is eternal, infinite, and always like itself. It is
equal and pure, without violent demonstrations: it is seen
with white hairs and is always young in the heart.

—HONORÉ DE BALZAC

The minute I heard my first love story,
I started looking for you, not knowing how blind that
    was.
Lovers don't finally meet somewhere.
They're in each other all along.

—MAULANA JALALU'DDIN RUMI

From *Letters to a Young Poet*
RAINER MARIE RILKE

To love is good, too: love being difficult. For one human
being to love another: that is perhaps the most difficult
of all our tasks, the ultimate, the last test and proof, the
work for which all other work is but preparation.

If you find it in your heart to care for somebody else,
you will have succeeded.

—MAYA ANGELOU

My Delight and Thy Delight
ROBERT BRIDGES

My delight and thy delight
Walking, like two angels white,
In the gardens of the night;

My desire and thy desire
Twining to a tongue of fire,
Leaping live, and laughing higher;

Thro' the everlasting strife
In the mysteries of life.
Love, from whom the world begun,
Hath the secret of the sun.

Love can tell, and love alone,
Whence the million stars were strewn
Why each atom knows its own,
How, in spite of woe and death,
Gay is life, and sweet is breath;

This he taught us, this we knew,
Happy in his science true,
Hand in hand as we stood
'Neath the shadows of the wood,
Heart to heart as we lay
In the dawning of the day.

From *The Divine Comedy*
DANTE

The love of God, unutterable and perfect, flows into a
pure soul the way light rushes into a transparent object.
The more love we receive, the more love we shine

forth; so that, as we grow clear and open, the more complete the joy of loving is. And the more souls who resonate together, the greater the intensity of their love for, mirror like, each soul reflects the other.

In the Month of May
ROBERT BLY

In the month of May when all leaves open,
I see when I walk how well all things
Lean on each other, how the bees work,
The fish make their living the first day.
Monarchs fly high; then I understand
I love you with what in me is unfinished.

I love you with what in me is still
Changing, what has no head or arms
Or legs, what has not found its body.
And why shouldn't the miraculous,
Caught on this earth, visit
The old man alone in his hut?

And why shouldn't Gabriel, who loves honey,
Be fed with our own radishes and walnuts?
And lovers, tough ones, how many there are
Whose holy bodies are not yet born.
Along the roads I see so many places
I would like us to spend the night.

Desire

There isn't a particle of you that I don't know, remember, and want.

—NOEL COWARD

Your words are my food, your breath my wine. You are everything to me.

—SARAH BERNHARDT

For it was not unto my ear you whispered, but into my heart. It was not my lips you kissed, but my soul.

—JUDY GARLAND

Thou art to me a delicious torment.

—RALPH WALDO EMERSON

Go, Lovely Rose
EDMUND WALLER

Go, lovely Rose—
Tell her that wastes her time and me,
That now she knows
When I resemble her to thee,
How sweet and fair she seems to be.

Tell her that's young,
And shuns to have her graces spied,

That hadst thou sprung
In deserts where no men abide,
Thou must have uncommended died.

Small is the worth
Of beauty from the light retired:
Bid her come forth,
Suffer herself to be desired,
And not blush so to be admired.

Then die—that she
The common fate of all things rare
May read in thee;
How small a part of time they share
That are so wondrous sweet and fair.

From *Ulysses*
JAMES JOYCE

I put my arms around him yes and drew him down to
me so he could feel my breasts all perfume yes and his
heart was going like mad and yes I said yes I will Yes.

To Celia
BEN JONSON

Drink to me only with thine eyes,
    And I will pledge with mine;

Or leave a kiss but in the cup
    And I'll not look for wine.
The thirst that from the soul doth rise
    Doth ask a drink divine;
But might I of Jove's nectar sup,
    I would not change for thine.

I sent thee late a rosy wreath,
    Not so much honoring thee
As giving it a hope that there it could not withered be;
But thou thereon didst only breathe,
    And sent'st it back to me;
Since when it grows, and smells, I swear,
    Not of itself but thee!

From *David Copperfield*
CHARLES DICKENS

If I may so express it, I was steeped in Dora. I was not merely over head and ears in love with her, but I was saturated through and through. Enough love might have been wrung out of me, metaphorically speaking, to drown anybody in; and yet there would have remained enough within me, and all over me, to pervade my entire existence.

Promises

Song of Songs 8:6

Let me be a seal upon our heart,
Like the seal upon your hand.

As for me, to love you alone, to make you happy, to do
nothing which would contradict your wishes, this is my
destiny and the meaning of my life.

—NAPOLEON BONAPARTE

I am, in every thought of my heart, yours.

—WOODROW WILSON

From *Beauty and the Beast*
MADAME LEPRINCE DE BEAUMONT
Translated by Alfred and Mary Elizabeth David

From this moment on, I give you my hand and I swear
that I shall be yours alone.

From *The Book and the Brotherhood*
IRIS MURDOCH

...I hereby give myself. I love you. You are the only
being whom I can love absolutely with my complete

self, with all my flesh and mind and heart. You are my mate, my perfect partner, and I am yours...It was a marvel that we ever met. It is some kind of divine luck that we are together now...As we look at each other we verify, we *know*, the perfection of our love, we *recognize* each other.

From *An Old Man's Love*
ANTHONY TROLLOPE

To me you are everything. I have been thinking as I walked up and down the path there, of all that I could do to make you happy. And I was so happy myself in feeling that I had your happiness to look after. How should I not let the wind blow too coldly on you? How should I be watchful to see that nothing should ruffle your spirits? What duties, what pleasures, what society should I provide for you?

From *Illuminata*
MARIANNE WILLIAMSON

With this ring, I give you my promise that from this
  day forward you shall not walk alone.
May my heart be your shelter and my arms be your
  home.

May God bless you always.
May we walk together through all things.
May you feel deeply loved, for indeed you are.
May you always see your innocence in my eyes.
With this ring, I give you my heart. I have no greater
    gift to give.
I promise I shall do my best
I shall always try,
I feel so honored to call you my husband/wife,
I feel so blessed to call you mine.
May we feel this joy forever.
I thank God.
I thank you.
Amen.

Hosea 2:21-22

I betroth you to me forever; I betroth you to me with
steadfast love and compassion; I betroth you to me in
faithfulness.

Sensual pleasure passes and vanishes in the twinkling of
an eye, but the friendship between us, the mutual confidence, the delights of the heart, the enchantment of
the soul, these things do not perish and can never be
destroyed. I shall love you until I die.

—VOLTAIRE

Partnership and Togetherness

We are shaped and fashioned by what we love.

—JOHANN WOLFGANG VON GOETHE

From every human being there rises a light that reaches straight to heaven. When two souls who are destined for each other find one another, their streams of light flow together and a single brighter light goes forth from their united being.

—BA'AL SHEM TOV

Two distincts,
division none.

—WILLIAM SHAKESPEARE

It is a rock of comfort to have your love and companionship at my side.

—WINSTON CHURCHILL to Clementine Churchill

You have so transformed my life that I can hardly remember what it felt like...before I knew you.

—CLEMENTINE CHURCHILL to Winston Churchill

Love is the condition in which the happiness of another person is essential to your own.

—ROBERT HEINLEIN

Vidyapati (Hindu love poem)
Translated by Edward C. Dimock, Jr. and
Denise Levertov

As the mirror to my hand,
The flowers to my hair,
Kohl to my eyes,
Tambul to my mouth
Musk to my breast
Necklace to my throat,
Ecstasy to my flesh,
Heart to my home—

As wing to bird,
Water to fish,
Life to the living—
So you to me.

From *The Prophet*
KAHLIL GIBRAN

You were born together, and together you shall be
    forevermore.
You shall be together when the wings of death scatter
    your days.
Ay, you shall be together even in your silent memory.
But let there be spaces in your togetherness,
And let the winds of the heavens dance between you.

Love one another, but make not a bondage of love:
Let it rather be a moving sea between the shores of
    your souls.
Fill each other's cup but drink not from one cup.
Give one another of your bread but eat not from the
    same loaf.
Sing and dance together and be joyous, but let each
    one of you
    be alone,
Even as the strings of a lute are alone though they
    quiver with
    the same music.

Give your hearts, but not into each other's keeping.
For only the hand of Life can contain your hearts.
And stand together yet not too near together:
For the pillars of the temple stand apart,
And the oak tree and the cypress grow not in each
    other's
    shadow.

Book of Ruth 1: 16-17

For whither thou goest, I will go;
And where thou lodgest, I will lodge;
Thy people shall be my people;
And thy God my God

Grow old along with me!
The best is yet to be.

— ROBERT BROWNING

To Be One with Each Other
GEORGE ELIOT

What greater thing is there for two human souls
than to feel that they are joined together to strengthen
each other in all labor, to minister to each other in all
    sorrow,
to share with each other in all gladness,
to be one with each other in the
silent unspoken memories?

Love's Philosophy
PERCY BYSSHE SHELLEY

The Fountains mingle with the River
And the Rivers with the Ocean,
The winds of Heaven mix for ever
With a sweet emotion;
Nothing in the world is single;
All things by a law divine
In one another's being mingle.
Why not I with thine?

See the mountains kiss high Heaven
And the waves clasp one another;
No sister-flower would be forgiven
If it disdained its brother,
And the sunlight clasps the earth
And the moonbeams kiss the sea:
What are all these kissings worth
If thou kiss not me?

The Passionate Shepherd to His Love
CHRISTOPHER MARLOWE

Come live with me and be my love,
And we will all the pleasures prove
That valleys, groves, hills, and fields,
Woods, or steep mountain yields.

And we will sit upon the rocks,
Seeing the shepherds feed their flocks,
By shallow rivers to whose falls
Melodious birds sing madrigals.

And I will make thee beds of roses
And a thousand fragrant posies,
A cap of flowers, and a kirtle
Embroidered all with leaves of myrtle;

A gown made of the finest wool
Which from our pretty lambs we pull;
Fair lined slippers for the cold,
With buckles of the purest gold;

A belt of straw and ivy buds,
With coral clasps and amber studs:
And if these pleasures may thee move,
Come live with me, and be my love.

The shepherd swains shall dance and sing
For thy delight each May morning:
If these delights thy mind may move,
Then live with me and be my love.

From *First Poems*
RAINER MARIA RILKE

Understand, I'll slip quietly
Away from the noisy crowd
When I see the pale
Stars rising, blooming over the oaks.

I'll pursue solitary pathways
Through the pale twilit meadows,
With only this one dream:
You come too.

From *Song of the Open Road*

WALT WHITMAN

Afoot and lighthearted, take to the open road,
Healthy, free, the world before you,
The long brown path before you, leading wherever you
    choose.
Say only to one another:
Camerado, I give you my hand!
I give you my love, more precious than money,
I give you myself before preaching or law:
Will you give me yourself?
Will you come travel with me?
Shall we stick by each other as long as we live?

Ecclesiastes 4:9-12

Two are better than one; because they have a good
reward for their labour. For if they fall, the one will lift
up his fellow: but woe to him that is alone when he fall-
eth; for he hath not another to help him up. Again, if
two lie together, then they have heat: but how can one
be warm alone? And if one prevail against him, two
shall withstand him; and a threefold cord is not quickly
broken.

Matthew 19:4-6

He answered, "Have you not read that he who made them from the beginning made them male and female and said, for this cause shall a man leave father and mother, and shall cleave to his wife: and they twain shall be one flesh? Wherefore they are no more twain, but one flesh. What therefore God hath joined together, let not man put asunder."

From *Chamber Music,* Poem XIII
JAMES JOYCE

Go seek her out all courteously,
And say I come,
Wind of spices whose song is ever
Epithalamium.
O, hurry over the dark lands
And run upon the sea
For seas and land shall not divide us
My love and me.

Now, wind, of your good courtesy
I pray you go,
And come into her little garden
And sing at her window;
Singing: The bridal wind is blowing

For Love is at his noon;
And soon will your true love be with you,
Soon, O soon.

From *Ceremonials*
JOHN DONNE

...so much one are you two...

Love Song
WILLLIAM CARLOS WILLIAMS

Sweep the house clean,
Hang fresh curtains
In the windows
Put on a new dress
And come with me!
The elm is scattering
Its little loaves
Of sweet smells
From a white sky!
Who shall hear of us
In the time to come?
Let him say there was
A burst of fragrance
From black branches.

Two souls with but a single thought, two hearts that
beat as one.

—FRIEDRICH HALM

From *Rubaiyat*
OMAR KHAYYÁM
Translated by Edward FitzGerald

A book of Verses underneath the Bough,
A Jug of Wine, a Loaf of Bread—and Thou
    Beside me singing in the Wilderness—
Oh, Wilderness were Paradise now!

Fulfillment
WILLIAM CAVENDISH

There is no happier life
    But in a wife;
The comforts are so sweet
    When two do meet.
'Tis plenty, peace, a calm
    Like dropping balm;
Love's weather is so fair,
    Like perfumed air.
Each word such pleasure brings
    Like soft-touched strings;

Love's passion moves the heart
    On either part;
Such harmony together,
    So pleased in either.
No discords; concords still;
    Sealed with one will.
By love, God made man one,
    Yet not alone.
Like stamps of king and queen
    It may be seen:
Two figures on one coin,
    So do they join,
Only they not embrace.
    We, face to face.

We Two, How Long We Were Fool'd
WALT WHITMAN

We two, how long we were fool'd,
Now transmuted, we swiftly escape as Nature escapes,
We are Nature, long have we been absent, but now we
    return,
We become plants, trunks, foliage, roots, bark,
We are bedded in the ground, we are rocks,
We are oaks, we grow in the openings side by side,
We browse, we are two among the wild herds
    spontaneous as any,

We are two fishes swimming in the sea together,
We are what locust blossoms are, we drop scent
around lanes mornings and evenings,
We are also the coarse smut of beasts, vegetables,
minerals,
We are two predatory hawks, we soar above and look
down,
We are two resplendent suns, we it is who balance
ourselves orbit and stellar, we are as two comets,
We prowl fang'd and four-footed in the woods, we
spring on prey,
We are two clouds for noons and afternoons driving
overhead,
We are seas mingling, we are two of those cheerful
waves rolling over each other and interwetting each
other,
We are what the atmosphere is, transparent, receptive,
pervious, impervious,
We are snow, rain, cold, darkness, we are each product
and influence of the globe,
We have circled and circled till we have arrived home
again, we two,
We have voided all but freedom and all but our own
joy.

somewhere I have never travelled...
E.E. CUMMINGS

somewhere I have never travelled,gladly beyond
any experience,youreyes have their silence:
in your most frail gesture are things which enclose me,
or which I cannot touch because theyare too near

your slightest look easily will unclose me
though I have closed myself as fingers,
you open always petal by petal myself as spring opens
(touching skilfully,mysteriously)her first rose

or if your wish be to close me,I and
my life will shut very beautifully,suddenly,
as when the heart of this flower imagines
the snow carefully everywhere descending;

nothing which we are to perceive in this world equals
the power of your intense fragility:whose texture
compels me with the colour of its countries,
rendering death and forever with each breathing

(i do not know what it is about you that closes
and opens;only something in me undersands
the voice of your eyes is deeper than all roses)
nobody,not even the rain,has such small hands

: III :

Having a Coke with You
FRANK O'HARA

is even more fun than going to San Sebastian, Irun,
    Hendaye,
    Biarritz, Bayonne
or being sick to my stomach on the Travesera de
    Gracia in
    Barcelona
partly because in your orange shirt you look like a
    better happier
    St. Sebastian
partly because of my love for you, partly because of
    your love for
    yoghurt
partly because of the fluorescent orange tulips around
    the birches
partly because of the secrecy our smiles take on before
    people
    and statuary
it is hard to believe when I'm with you that there can be
    anything as still
as solemn as unpleasantly definitive as statuary when
    right in
    front of it
in the warm New York 4 o'clock light we are drifting
    back and
    forth

between each other like a tree breathing through its
    spectacles

and the portrait show seems to have no faces in it at
    all, just
    paint
you suddenly wonder why in the world anyone ever did
    them
    I look
at you and I would rather look at you than all the
    portraits in
    the world
except possibly for the *Polish Rider* occasionally and
    anyway it's in
    the Frick
which thank heavens you haven't gone to yet so we can
    go
    together the first time
and the fact that you move so beautifully more or less
    takes care
    of Futurism
just as at home I never think of the *Nude Descending
    a Staircase*
    or
at a rehearsal a single drawing of Leonardo or
    Michelangelo that
    used to wow me

and what good does all the research of the Impression-
    ists do
    them
when they never got the right person to stand near the
    tree when
    the sun sank
or for that matter Marino Marini when he didn't pick
    the rider
    as carefully
    as the horse
it seems they were all cheated of some marvelous
    experience
which is not going to go wasted on me which is why
    I'm telling
    you about it

i carry your heart with me
E.E. CUMMINGS

i carry your heart with me(i carry it in
my heart)i am never without it(anywhere
i go you go,my dear; and whatever is done
by only me is your doing,my darling)
                    i fear
no fate(for you are my fate,my sweet)i want
no world(for beautiful you are my world,my true)

and it's you are whatever a moon has always meant
and whatever a sun will always sing is you

here is the deepest secret nobody knows
(here is the root of the root and the bud of the bud
and the sky of the sky of a tree called life;which grows
higher than the soul can hope or mind can hide)
and this is the wonder that's keeping the stars apart

i carry your heart(i carry it in my heart)

From *Variations on the Word* Sleep
MARGARET ATWOOD

I would like to be the air
that inhabits you for a moment
only. I would like to be that unnoticed
and that necessary

Never above you. Never below you. Always beside you.
—WALTER WINCHELL

From every human being there rises a light that reaches
straight to heaven. And when two souls, destined to be
together, find each other, the streams of light flow together and a single brighter light goes forth from their
united being.

—BA'AL SHEM TOV

I am the words and you are the melody, I am the melody and you are the words.

— HINDU MANTRA

"Always Return" from *The Couple's Tao Te Ching*
LAU TZU
Interpreted by William Martin

It is good to know your strength
But always return to your flexibility.
If you can cradle your beloved in your arms
in nurturing gentleness,
love will flow through you.

It is good to achieve things
But always return to anonymity.
Your beloved does not need your achievements
But needs your uncomplicated soul.

It is good to work for change,
But always return to what is.
If you accept all things whether painful or joyful,
You will always know
That you belong to each other
And to the Tao.

May our minds move in accord. May our thinking be in harmony—common the purpose and common the desire. May our prayers and worship be alike, and may our devotional offerings be one and the same.

—RIG VEDA

Thee lift me, and I'll lift thee, and we'll ascend together.

—QUAKER PROVERB

The true beloveds of this world are in their lovers' eyes lilacs opening, ship lights, school bells, a landscape, remembered conversations, friends, a child's Sunday, lost voices, one's favorite suit, autumn and all seasons.

—TRUMAN CAPOTE

From *Winnie the Pooh*
A.A. MILNE

If you live to be a hundred, I want to live to be a hundred minus one day so I never have to live without you.

In love, one and one are one.

—JEAN PAUL SARTRE

From *Love Song*
RAINER MARIA RILKE

Everything that touches us, me and you, takes us together like a violin's bow, which draws one voice out of
two separate strings.
Upon what instrument are we two spanned? And what
musician holds us in his hand? Oh sweetest song.

Destiny
SIR EDWIN ARNOLD

Somewhere there waiteth in this world of ours
For one lone soul another lonely soul,
Each choosing each through all the weary hours
And meeting strangely at one sudden goal.
Then blend they, like green leaves with golden flowers,
Into one beautiful and perfect whole;
And life's long night is ended, and the way
Lies open onward to eternal day.

Marriage

If there is such a thing as a good marriage,
it is because it resembles friendship rather
than love.

—MICHEL DE MONTAIGNE

From *The Chuppah*
MARGE PIERCY

O my love O my love we dance
Under the chuppah standing over us
Like an animal on its four legs,
Like a table on which we set our love
As a feast, like a tent
Under which we work
Not safe but no longer solitary
In the searing heat of our time.

From *The Irrational Season*
MADELEINE L'ENGLE

But ultimately there comes a moment when a decision
must be made. Ultimately two people who love each
other must ask themselves how much they hope for
as their love grows and deepens, and how much risk
they are willing to take...It is indeed a fearful gamble...
Because it is the nature of love to create, a marriage
itself is something which has to be created, so that,
together we become a new creature.

   To marry is the biggest risk in human relations that
a person can take...If we commit ourselves to one person for life this is not, as many people think, a rejection
of freedom; rather it demands the courage to move into

all the risks of freedom, and the risk of love which is permanent; into that love which is not possession, but participation...It takes a lifetime to learn another person...When love is not possession, but participation, then it is part of that co-creation which is our human calling, and which implies such risk that it is often rejected.

I'd be crazy to propose to her, but when I see that profile of hers I feel the only thing worth doing in the world is to grab her and start shouting for clergymen and bridesmaids to come running.

— P.G. WODEHOUSE

The Marriage Ceremony
WILLIAM WORDSWORTH

The Vested priest before the altar stands:
Approach, come gladly, ye prepared, in sight
Of God and chosen friends, your troth to plight
With the symbolic ring, and willing hands
Solemnly joined. Now sanctify the bands
O father!— to the espoused thy blessing give,
That mutually assisted they may live
Obedient, as here taught, to thy commands.
So prays the church, to consecrate a vow
"The which would endless matrimony make;"

Union that shadows forth and doth partake
A mystery potent human love to endow
With heavenly, each more prized for the other's sake;
weep not, meek Bride! Uplift thy timid brow.

The Owl and the Pussy-Cat

EDWARD LEAR

The Owl and the Pussy-Cat went to sea
    In a beautiful pea-green boat.
They took some honey, and plenty of money
    Wrapped up in a five-pound note.
The Owl looked up to the stars above,
    And sang to a small guitar,
"O lovely Pussy! O Pussy, my love,
What a beautiful Pussy you are,
      You are,
      You are!
What a beautiful Pussy you are!"

Pussy said to the Owl, "You elegant fowl!
    How charmingly sweet you sing!
O let us be married! too long we have tarried:
    But what shall we do for a ring?"
They sailed away, for a year and a day,
    To the land where the Bong-Tree grows,
And there in a wood a Piggy-wig stood,

With a ring at the end of his nose,
    His nose,
    His nose!
With a ring at the end of his nose.

"Dear Pig, are you willing to sell for one shilling
    Your ring?" Said the Piggy, "I will."
So they took it away, and were married next day
    By the Turkey who lives on the hill.
They dined on mince, and slices of quince,
    Which they ate with a runcible spoon;
And hand in hand, on the edge of the sand
    They danced by the light of the moon,
        The moon,
        The moon,
They danced by the light of the moon.

Marriage Morning
LORD ALFRED TENNYSON

Light, so low upon earth,
    You send a flash to the sun.
Here is the golden close of love,
    All my wooing is done.
Oh, the woods and the meadows,
    Woods, where we hid from the wet,
Stiles where we stayed to be kind,
    Meadows in which we met!

Light, so low in the vale
  You flash and lighten afar,
For this is the golden morning of love,
  And you are his morning star.
Flash, I am coming, I come,
  By meadow and stile and wood,
Oh, lighten into my eyes and my heart,
  Into my heart and my blood!
Heart, are you great enough
  For a love that never tires?
O heart, are you great enough for love?
  I have heard of thorns and briers.
Over the thorns and briers,
  Over the meadows and stiles,
Over the world to the end of it
  Flash for a million miles.

Men Marry What They Need
JOHN CIARDI

Men marry what they need. I marry you,
morning by morning, day by day, night by night,
and every marriage makes this marriage new.

In the broken name of heaven, in the light
that shatters granite, but the spitting shore,
in air that leaps and wobbles like a kite,

I marry you from time and a great door
is shut and stays shut against wind, sea, stone,
sunburst, and heavenfall. And home once more

inside our walls of skin and struts of bone,
man-woman, woman-man, and each the other,
I marry you by all dark and all dawn

and have my laugh at death. Why should I bother
the flies about me? Let them buzz and do.
Men marry their queen, their daughter, or their mother

by hidden names, but that thin buzz whines through:
where reasons are no reason, cause is true.
Men marry what they need. I marry you.

Facing The Future
NATHANIEL HAWTHORNE

Methinks this birthday of our married life is like a cape,
which we now have doubled, and find a more intimate
ocean of love stretching out before us. God bless us
and keep us; for there is something more awful in happiness than in sorrow—the latter being composed of
the texture and substance of eternity, so that spirits still
embodied may well tremble at it.

Tin Wedding Whistle

OGDEN NASH

Though you know it anyhow
Listen to me, darling, now

Proving what I need not prove
How I know I love you, love.

Near and far, near and far,
I am happy where you are;

Likewise I have never learnt
How to be it where you aren't.

Far and wide, far and wide,
I can walk with you beside;

Furthermore, I tell you what,
I sit and sulk where you are not.

Visitors remark my frown
When you're upstairs and I am down,

Yes, and I'm afraid I pout
When I'm indoors and you are out;

But how contentedly I view
Any room containing you.

In fact, I care not where you be,
Just as long as it's with me.

In all your absences I glimpse
Fire and flood and trolls and imps.

Is your train a minute slothful?
I goad the stationmaster wrothful.

When with friends to bridge you drive
I never know if you're alive,

And when you linger late in shops
I long to telephone the cops.

Yet how worth the waiting for,
To see you coming through the door.

Somehow, I can be complacent
Never but with you adjacent.

Near and far, near and far,
I am happy where you are;

Likewise I have never learnt
How to be it where you aren't

Then grudge me not my fond endeavor,
To hold you in my sight forever;

Let none, not even you, disparage
Such valid reason for a marriage.

Husbands and Wives, Men and Women

From *Bring Me a Unicorn*

ANNE MORROW LINDBERGH (on her impending marriage to Charles Lindbergh)

Don't wish me happiness—it's gotten beyond that somehow. Wish me courage and strength and a sense of humor—I will need them all...

From *Wuthering Heights*

EMILY BRONTË

...He's more myself than I am. Whatever our souls are made of, his and mine are the same...He's always, always in my mind; not as a pleasure to myself, but as my own being.

To Julia

ROBERT HERRICK

Julia, I bring
To thee this ring,
Made for thy finger fit;
To show by this
That our love is
Or should be, like to it.

Loose though it be,
The joint is free;
So, when love's yoke is on,
It must not gall,
Nor fret at all,
With hard oppression.

But it must play,
Still either way,
And be, too, such a yoke
As not too wide
To overslide,
Or be so straight to choke.

So we who bear
This beam, must rear
Ourselves to such a height
As that the stay
Of either may
Create the burthen light.

And as this round
Is nowhere found
To flaw, or else to sever,
So let our love
As endless prove
As pure as gold forever.

From *Beloved*

TONI MORRISON

She is a friend of my mind. She gather me, man. The
pieces I am, she gather them and give them back to me
in all the right order. It's good, you know, when you got
a woman who is a friend of your mind.

She Walks In Beauty

GEORGE GORDON, LORD BYRON

She walks in Beauty, like the night
Of cloudless climes and starry skies;
And all that's best of dark and bright
Meet in her aspect and her eyes:
Thus mellow'd to that tender light
Which heaven to gaudy day denies.

One shade the more, one ray the less
Had half impair'd the nameless grace
Which waves in every raven tress,
Or softly lightens o'er her face;
Where thoughts serenely sweet express
How pure, how dear their dwelling place.

And on that cheek, and o'er that brow,
So soft, so calm yet eloquent,
The smiles that win, the tints that glow,

But tell of days in goodness spent,
A mind at peace with all below,
A heart whose love is innocent.

From *To His Wife Mary*
WILLIAM WORDSWORTH

Every day every hour every moment makes me feel
more deeply how blessed we are in each other, how
purely how faithfully how ardently, and how tenderly
we love each other; I put this last word last because,
though I am persuaded that a deep affection is not un-
common in married life, yet I am confident that a lively,
gushing, thought-employing, spirit-stirring, passion of
love is very rare even among good people...O Mary I
love you with a passion of love which grows 'til I tremble to think of its strength.

Proverbs 18:22

Whoso findeth a wife findeth a good thing, and obtain-
eth favour of the LORD.

A Dedication to my Wife

T.S. ELIOT

To whom I owe the leaping delight
That quickens my senses in our waking time
And the rhythm that governs the repose of our
    sleeping time,
The breathing in unison
Of lovers whose bodies smell of each other
Who think the same thoughts without need of speech
And babble the same speech without need of meaning.

No peevish winter wind shall chill
No sullen tropic sun shall wither
The roses in the rose-garden which is ours and ours
    only.

But this dedication is for others to read:
These are private words addressed to you in public.

From *Jane Eyre*

CHARLOTTE BRONTË

Mr. Rochester proposes to Jane:
"I offer you my hand, my heart, and a share of all my
possessions....
I ask you to pass through life at my side—to be my second self and best earthly companion....Come to my

side, Jane and let us explain and understand one another...I summon you as my wife: it is you only I intend
to marry...Come to me—come to me entirely now," he
said, and added in his deepest tone, speaking in my ear
as his cheek was laid on mine, "Make my happiness—I
will make yours."

To Celia

SIR CHARLES SEDLEY

Not, Celia that I juster am,
    Or better than the rest!
For I would change each hour like them,
    Were not my heart at rest.

But I am tied to very thee
    By every thought I have;
Thy face I only care to see,
    Thy heart I only crave.

All that in woman is adored
    In thy dear self I find;
For the whole sex can but afford
    The handsome and the kind.

Why then should I seek further store
    And still make love anew?
When change itself can give no more,
    'Tis easy to be true.

To My Dear and Loving Husband
ANNE BRADSTREET

If ever two were one, then surely we.
If ever man were loved by wife, then thee;
If ever wife was happy in a man,
Compare with me, ye women, if you can.
I prize thy love more than whole mines of gold
Or all the riches that the East doth hold.
My love is such that rivers cannot quench,
Nor ought but love from thee, give recompense.
Thy love is such I can no way repay,
The heavens reward thee manifold, I pray.
Then while we live, in love let's so persevere
That when we live no more, we may live ever.

Summum Bonum
ROBERT BROWNING

All the breath and the bloom of the
        year in the bag of one bee:
    All the wonder and wealth of the mine in
        the heart of one gem:
In the core of one pearl all the shade and the
        shine of the sea:
    Breath and bloom, shade and shine,—wonder,
        wealth, and—how far above them—

Truth, that's bright than gem,
   Trust, that's purer than pearl,—
Brightest truth, purest trust in the universe—
      all were for me
      in the kiss of one girl.

Jenny Kiss'd Me
LEIGH HUNT

Jenny kissed me when we met,
Jumping from the chair she sat in.
Time, you thief! Who love to get
Sweets into your list, put that in.
Say I'm weary, say I'm sad;
Say that health and wealth have missed me;
Say I'm growing old, but add—
Jenny kissed me.

They are not said to be husband and wife, who merely
sit together. Rather they alone are called husband and
wife, who have one soul in two bodies.

— GURU AMAR DAS

Let us be grateful to people who make us happy; they
are the charming gardeners who make our souls blossom.

— MARCEL PROUST

...she gets into the remotest recesses of my heart, and shines all through me.

—NATHANIEL HAWTHORNE

~~~~~~

The Past and the Future

What lies behind us, and what lies before us are tiny matters compared to what lies within us.

—RALPH WALDO EMERSON

The First Day
CHRISTINA ROSSETTI

I wish I could remember the first day,
First hour, first moment of your meeting me;
If bright or dim the season, it might be
Summer or winter for aught I can say.
So unrecorded did it slip away,
So blind was I to see and to forsee,
So dull to mark the budding of my tree
That would not blossom yet for many a May.

If only I could recollect it! Such
A day of days! I let it come and go
As traceless as a thaw of bygone snow.

It seemed to mean so little, meant so much!
If only now I could recall that touch,
First touch of hand in hand!—Did one but know.

When You Are Old
W.B. YEATS

When you are old and gray and full of sleep,
And nodding by the fire, take down this book,
And slowly read, and dream of the soft look
Your eyes had once, and of their shadows deep;

How many loved your moments of glad grace,
And loved your beauty with love false or true,
But one man loved the pilgrim soul in you,
And loved the sorrows of your changing face;

And bending down beside the glowing bars,
Murmur, a little sadly, how Love fled,
And paced upon the mountains far above,
And hid his face amid a crowd of stars.

One Day I Wrote Her Name Upon the Strand
EDMUND SPENSER

One day I wrote her name upon the strand,
But came the waves and washèd it away:
Again I wrote it with a second hand,

But came the tide and made my pains his prey.
Vain man (said she) that dost in vain assay
A mortal thing so to immortalise;
For I myself shall like to this decay,
And eke my name be wipèd out likewise.
Not so (quod I); let baser things devise
To die in dust, but you shall live by fame;
My verse your virtues rare shall eternise,
And in the heavens write your glorious name:
    Where, when as Death shall all the world subdue,
    Our love shall live, and later life renew.

Now!

ROBERT BROWNING

Out of your whole life give but a moment!
    All of your life that has gone before,
    All to come after it,—so you ignore,
So you make perfect the present; condense,
In a rapture of rage, for perfection's endowment,
Thought and feeling and soul and sense,
Merged in a moment which gives me at last
You around me for once, you beneath me, above me—
Me, sure that, despite of time future, time past,
This tick of life-time's one moment you love me!

How long such suspension may linger? Ah, Sweet,
    The moment eternal—just that and no more—
    When ecstasy's utmost we clutch at the core,
While cheeks burn, arms open, eyes shut, and lips
    meet!

Believe Me, If All Those Endearing Young Charms
THOMAS MOORE

Believe me, if all those endearing young charms,
    Which I gaze on so fondly to-day,
Were to change to tomorrow, and fleet in my arms,
    Like fairy-gifts fading away,
Thou wouldst still be adored, as this moment thou art,
    Let thy loveliness fade as it will,
And around the dear ruin each wish of my heart
    Would entwine itself verdantly still.

It is not while beauty and youth are thine own,
    And thy cheeks unprofaned by a tear,
That the fervor and faith of a soul may be known,
    To which time will but make thee more dear!
No, the heart that has truly loved never forgets,
    But as truly loves on to the close,
As the sunflower turns to her god when he sets
    The same look which she turned when he rose!

He Wishes For The Cloths of Heaven
W.B. YEATS

Had I the heavens' embroidered cloths,
Enwrought with golden and silver light,
The blue and the dim and the dark cloths
Of night and light and the half light,
I would spread the cloths under your feet:
But I, being poor, have only my dreams;
I have spread my dreams under your feet;
Tread softly because you tread on my dreams.

~~~~~~

Love Letters

You have the great gift of understanding, Mary. You are like the Great Spirit, who befriends man not only to share his life, but to add to it. My knowing you is the greatest thing in my days and nights, a miracle quite outside the natural order of things.

— KAHLIL GIBRAN to Mary Haskell

Without you, dearest dearest I couldn't see or hear or feel or think—or live—I love you so and I'm never in all our lives going to let us be apart another night.

— ZELDA FITZGERALD to F. Scott Fitzgerald

It is incredible how essential to me you have become.
—VITA SACKVILLE-WEST to Virginia Woolf

My angel, my all, my very self.
Is not our love truly founded in Heaven—and, what is
more, as strongly cemented as the firmament of
heaven?
ever yours
ever mine
ever ours

—LUDWIG VAN BEETHOVEN
to the "Immortal Beloved"

You are all about me—I seem to breathe you—hear
you—feel you in me and of me....We two, you know
have everything before us, and we shall do very great
things—I have perfect faith in us—and so perfect is my
love for you that I am, as it were, still, silent to my very
soul. I want nobody but you for my lover and my friend
and to nobody but you shall I be faithful.
—KATHERINE MANSFIELD to John Middleton Murry

The air is full of the music of your voice, my soul and
body seem no longer mine, but mingled in some exqui-
site ecstasy with yours. I feel incomplete without you.
—OSCAR WILDE to Constance Wilde

...my heart beats through my entire body and is conscious only of you. I belong to you; there is really no other way of expressing it, and that is not strong enough.

—FRANZ KAFKA to Felice Bauer

When I saw you I thought, here is a man I could love. And I was no longer afraid of feelings.

—ANAÏS NIN to Henry Miller

My dear Girl I love you ever and ever and without reserve. The more I have known you the more have I lov'd.... You are always new. The last of your kisses was ever the sweetest; the last smile the brightest; the last movement the gracefullest.

—JOHN KEATS to Fanny Brawne

My love for you tonight is so deep and tender that it seems to be outside myself as well. I am fast shut up like a little lake in the embrace of some big mountains, you would see me down below, deep and shining—and quite fathomless, my dear. You might drop your heart into me and you'd never hear it touch bottom. I love you—I love you.

—KATHERINE MANSFIELD to John Middleton Murry

...the thought of you sings, smiles, shines, and dances like a joyous fire that gives out a thousand colours and penetrating warmth.

— GUSTAVE FLAUBERT to Louise Colet

Words can never tell you, however, —form them, transform them anyway, —how perfectly dear you are to me—perfectly dear to my heart and soul. I look back, and in every one point, every word and gesture, every letter, every silence – you have been entirely perfect to me—I would not change one word, one look.

— ROBERT BROWNING to Elizabeth Barrett

Love me always, love me always. You have been the supreme, the perfect love of my life; there can be no other...O sweetest of all boys, most loved of all loves, my soul clings to your soul, my life is your life, and in all the world of pain and pleasure you are my ideal of admiration and joy.

— OSCAR WILDE to Lord Alfred Douglas

My greatest good fortune in a life of brilliant experiences has been to find you, and to lead my life with you.

— WINSTON CHURCHILL to Clementine Churchill

God must think a lot of me to have given me you.

— GROVER CLEVELAND ALEXANDER to his wife Aimee

My heart is yours—my thoughts—myself.

> — Letter from JOHN RUSKIN to Effie Gray

...That you should be the one woman to me of all women; that my hunger for you should be greater than any hunger for food I have ever felt; that my desire for you should bite harder than any other desire I have ever felt for fame and fortune and such things;—all, all goes to show how big is this our love.... Ah Love, it looms large. It fills my whole horizon. Wherever I look I feel you, see you, touch you, and know my need for you...I love you, you only and wholly. And there are no joys of a future life to make of less value the joy I know and shall know through you.

> —JACK LONDON to Charmian Kittredge

FURTHER READING

WHILE THERE ARE MANY inspirational books available on the subjects of love, marriage, and vows, the following are particularly recommended by the author for further reading:

Ackerman, Diane, and Mackin, Jeanne, ed. *The Book of Love.* New York: WW Norton & Co., 1998.

Hass, Robert, and Mitchell, Stephen. *Into The Garden A Wedding Anthology: Poetry and Prose on Love and Marriage.* New York: Harper Perennial, A division of Harper Collins Publishers, 1993.

Macomb, Rev. Susanna Stefanachi, with Thompson, Andrea. *Joining Hands and Hearts: Interfaith, Intercultural Wedding Celebrations.* New York: A Fireside Book, Simon & Schuster, 2003.

Munro, Eleanor. New York: Penguin Books, 1989.

CREDITS

RELIGIOUS AND SPIRITUAL VOWS

ACKNOWLEDGMENTS

MANY PEOPLE CONTRIBUTED their knowledge to the content of this book.

I would like to express my gratitude to the many religious leaders who provided insight and guidance regarding the vows and wedding traditions of their faith, particularly: Rabbi Richard F. Address, Union for Reform Judaism; Father John Matusiak, Orthodox Church in America; The Rev. Dr. Clayton L. Morris, Episcopal Church Center; Dr. B.V. Venkatakrishna Sastry, Hindu University of America; and Monsignor Anthony Sherman, United States Conference of Catholic Bishops.

I also extend thanks to the following individuals and organizations for their information and assistance: Habibe Ali, Islamic Society of North America; Chel Avery, Quaker Information Center; Sant Singh Khalsa, www.sikhnet.com; Anne Lyster, Humanist Society; Barb Porter, Abingdon Press; Stephen E. Scott, Elizabethtown College Young Center for Anabaptist and Pietist Studies; Ganden Thurman, Tibet House New York; and PresbyTel, the General Information Service for the Presbyterian Church.

I am once again grateful to have the opportunity to work with the wonderful team at Stewart, Tabori & Chang. Special thanks to publisher Leslie Stoker and to my editor Beth Huseman, whose keen observations, thoughtful suggestions, and unflappable nature are greatly appreciated. As always, it was a pleasure from start to finish. I would also like to thank the talented team at Studio Blue for their lovely design and ability to make sense of the many levels of information in this book.

On a personal note, I'd like to thank my husband Alan for making the effort to commit our wedding vows to memory with me on the last minute (whew!), and also Father Gerald Gunderson for making sure we delivered them without a hitch on the big day. Thanks to the friends and family who cheered us on.

And finally, with love to my parents and their vows of the past, and my daughter Violet and her vows someday in the future.

INDEX

: 155 :